CARL SANDBURG

CARL SANDBURG

A Pictorial Biography

by JOSEPH HAAS and GENE LOVITZ

G. P. Putnam's Sons, New York

To Elmer Gertz who, as his friend Carl Sandburg said of him, "fears no dragons."

Contents

Acknowledgments

WE are indebted to many people, libraries, institutions, and publications for their help, advice, and encouragement in the research and preparation for this book. Of course, we cannot list the names of everyone who has aided us, and of those we have overlooked, we can plead only for indulgence and understanding.

First, we must acknowledge our obligation to attorney Elmer Gertz, an old friend of Carl Sandburg, whose enthusiasm for this project sometimes outdistanced our own. Secondly, our gratitude is owed to Harry and Ruth Barnard, who first recognized the value of a book such as this and maintained an unwavering belief in it.

We wish we could cite the particular assistance each of the following people or organizations has provided to us. However, since they are aware of how useful their help was, at least we can offer our gratitude along with this alphabetical listing of their names:

Paul M. Angle, former director of the Chicago Historical Society; Juanita Bednar, president of the Carl Sandburg Association; Consul Eric Carlsson of Djursholm, Sweden, Carl Sandburg's cousin; Sven Dagermalm, keeper of the Archives, Vadstena, Sweden; Dean R. B. Downs, University of Illinois Library; William T. Evjue, editor and publisher of the Madison (Wisconsin) *Capital Times*; D. R. Fitzpatrick, editorial cartoonist, St. Louis *Post-Dispatch;* Severin Fredriksson, of Asbo, Sweden, an authority on Swedish folklore; Dr. Arthur W. Freese, of Chicago, an old friend of Carl Sandburg; the

9

Acknowledgments

Galesburg (Illinois) Police Department; Max M. Goodsill, public relations director of Knox College, Galesburg; Hans Hammarskiold, noted Swedish photographer; the Reverend John Harmansson, pastor, Allhelgona Parish, Vadstena, Sweden; Erwin Leiser, of Zurich, Switzerland, motion picture director and television producer; Craig E. Lovitt, Publicity and Alumni Office, Knox College; Edward N. MacConomy, Referral Library, Library of Congress; Jens Nyholm, director of the Northwestern University Library; the Reverend Ordell W. Peterson, pastor, First Lutheran Church, Galesburg; Martin Sandburg, Jr., nephew of Carl Sandburg; Dr. Lawrence W. Towner, director of the Newberry Library, Chicago; Arthur Witman, photographer, St. Louis *Post-Dispatch*; Jennings Wood, chief of the Exchange and Gift Division, Library of Congress; and J. E. Zuckerman, manager-director of the Hotel Custer, Galesburg.

In addition, we want to thank officials of the U. S. Embassy in Stockholm, the Swedish National Archives, and the Swedish Royal Consulate General in Chicago, as well as the librarians of the Chicago *Daily News* and of the Swedish newspapers *Dagens Nyheter* and *Svenska Dagbladet*.

Lastly, thanks are due our publisher, Walter J. Minton of Putnam's, for his patience and his invaluable editorial guidance.

Prologue

In a way it was a homecoming for the white-haired old man as he strode, sturdy and erect, down the ramp from the airliner that had just landed at Stockholm's Bromma Airport. A delegation of government officials, pressed by a crowd of reporters, photographers, television cameramen, and other welcomers, moved forward to greet him.

The old man acknowledged the excitement with his well-known widemouthed grin, and overwhelming pleasure brought out the blue in his normally smoke-gray eyes. *"Vad i hela min tidt!"* he exclaimed. What on earth was all the fuss about, and why were traveler and welcomers alike so exuberant over this arrival?

Perhaps it was because Carl Sandburg knew—and some members of the crowd recognized—the significance of his journey to Sweden. The aged poet, at eighty-one, was paying homage to the roots of his existence by making this visit to the homeland of his parents. Sandburg, hailed by two generations of critics as one of the truly valid voices of American literature, was acknowledging, by this pilgrimage, his debt to two lands—the Old World, as well as the New. To a life that was unquestionably an American saga, Sweden had provided the rich and solid prologue.

The Swedish exclamation had come easily and naturally to Sandburg's lips. In the humble frame house where he was born in Galesburg, Illinois, he had learned to say *Far* and *Mor* (Father

11

Carl Sandburg walks down the ramp from the airliner at Stockholm's Bromma Airport, August 6, 1959.

and Mother) before he had begun to speak English. When he was thirsty as a child, he had clamored, not for milk, but for *mjolk*.

As he had spoken the Swedish of his immigrant parents before he had begun to acquire the language of his native land, so, too, Sandburg had learned from them the values of an older culture before he had begun to adopt the standards of the young American society. The importance of honesty, diligence, thrift, love for the land, recognition of the dignity of labor, self-respect, and the value of a good name were to color his thinking long after a Swedish accent ceased to taint his speech. Sandburg was a spokesman for America, but this was as much because of his immigrant stock as it was in spite of it, for many of the values of American democracy were planted by the oppressed of Europe, whose yearnings and ideals had found the nourishment and climate to blossom in the vigorous soil of a new earth.

More than a century before Sandburg's brief and final visit to Sweden, his parents had emigrated from that nation as steerage passengers. Theirs had been only two more hopeful faces among the unprecedented multitude setting out for the newest promised land. But on this sunny day in August, 1959, Carl Sandburg was returning as a celebrity, a beloved poet and writer. He was to be the guest speaker at Swedish-American Day in Stockholm's Skansen Park, he was to be celebrated on a program broadcast over the national television network, and before his week's sojourn ended, he was to be summoned to the royal palace to accept Sweden's Litteris et Artibus Medal from King Gustav VI Adolf.

Such recognition for his achievements meant much to Sandburg, for unlike many famous people, he had never become cynical about popular acclaim. But Carl Sandburg had not come to Sweden in order to gather further laurels. No, he was there to visit two villages in the province of Ostergotland—the land of the Eastern Goths—southwest of Stockholm in a verdant farming area.

One was the village of Asbo where his father, Alfred Danielsson, had been born. Sandburg learned there from Severin Fredriksson (a Swedish writer) how Fredriksson's grandparents had helped Danielsson's family prepare, in 1856, for their six- to eight-week crossing to America as steerage passengers in a sailing vessel. Friends and neighbors had supplied Danielsson's parents, the Daniel Nilssons, with hard dark bread and dried lamb's meat to sustain them through the long voyage. Then, before the Nilssons boarded the ship, their friends had accompanied them to the church at Ekeby to pray that they would find in America the good life they were seeking and to sing together for the last time the songs and hymns of their native land.

With the exception of Fredriksson's story, there was little in Asbo to remind Sandburg of his Swedish roots. A laborer, Nilsson had never earned enough money to afford a house, and the family had lodged in rented quarters. So Sandburg, with his hunger for confirmation of his Swedish heritage, spent only a few hours in Asbo.

But not many miles away, in the village of Appuna on the shore of Lake Takern, his memories, acquired secondhand from his mother's nostalgic tales of her life in the old country, were affirmed.

Traveling in the motorcade of newsmen who followed Sandburg on this sentimental journey, the old poet arrived at the small farmhouse in Appuna where his mother, Clara Andersdotter, had lived. After he had been welcomed by the present owner, Olle Gustafsson, Sandburg strode into the house and walked slowly through room after room. It now had such modern conveniences as a refrigerator and indoor plumbing, but with its low ceilings and doorways and the forbidding neatness of its parlor, the house looked almost exactly the way Clara had described it to her little boy seventy-five years before.

"Oh, yes," Sandburg murmured. "There is the father's and mother's bedroom. And there is the kitchen backroom with the handloom, and the kids lived upstairs. And one was taught," he recalled, bending to go under a low portal, "to be polite because one had to bow in order to pass through the doors, so low are they."

After a thorough tour of the house, Sandburg returned to the farmyard for a respite from the highly emotional experience. Warming in the sunlight, he chatted with the villagers about farming. Yes, he told them, he was a farmer, too. Back at his home in North Carolina, he and his wife tended a prizewinning herd of goats on the slopes of Big Glassy Mountain. He talked with them about crops and cattle, and then he examined some old farm equipment in the yard, and perhaps this reminded him, again, of an earlier time.

Eyes hazing with tears, Sandburg excused himself and walked away from the villagers to be alone for a moment in the golden fields nearby. He bent to lift a handful of earth and crumbled it through his

The old poet's eyes haze with tears as he walks away from the villagers to be alone for a moment in the nearby fields.

fingers. "This is for me holy earth," he said, "and I am grateful to Providence that I got the opportunity to come here."

Then he visited the village church. The organist played a lovely old hymn about Sweden's brief summer, "In This Lovely Summertime," while Sandburg browsed through the church's ancient Bible, dating from the time of Charles XII. "Yes, yes," Sandburg said, proud of how much Swedish he remembered as he translated a favorite Psalm—"The Lord is my shepherd. . . ."—from the book's ornate illuminated lettering. When the Reverend Folke Odenbring brought out old church records that documented the genealogy of Sandburg's mother's family, Sandburg questioned him avidly about them until he had exhausted the pastor's knowledge of the subject. Leaving the church later, Sandburg paused to gaze across the fertile plain of Ostergotland, and he said, "It resembles Illinois, but it may be even prettier."

He paid another visit to his mother's home, where he stared intently at each room as if he wanted to engrave it on his memory. Then, before he left the house and Appuna for good, he halted before a mirror in the vestibule to study his face and to ask himself, "What on earth do you lack, boy?" A long, slow smile was his answer.

Sandburg, age eighty-one, and his famous brother-in-law, photography pioneer Edward Steichen, age eighty, are welcomed by the Swedish press at Bromma Airport after completing a goodwill trip to Moscow for the United States Information Agency. In Moscow they had opened Steichen's "Family of Man" photography exhibit.

Carl Sandburg's mother, Clara Mathilda Andersdotter (1850–1926), and his father, Alfred Danielsson (1846–1910), before he changed his name to August Sandburg.

A typical farmland scene in the land of his parents—the fertile province of Ostergottland.

Carl Sandburg in the church his mother had attended, Appuna, Sweden, August 11, 1959.

LEFT *Carl Sandburg studies the material for his appearance on Swedish television with Erwin Leiser, well-known European television and film producer-director.*

RIGHT *Carl Sandburg after his visit with King Gustav VI Adolf. In his hand he carries the Litteris et Artibus Medal presented to him by the king for accomplishments in fine arts, August 15, 1959.*

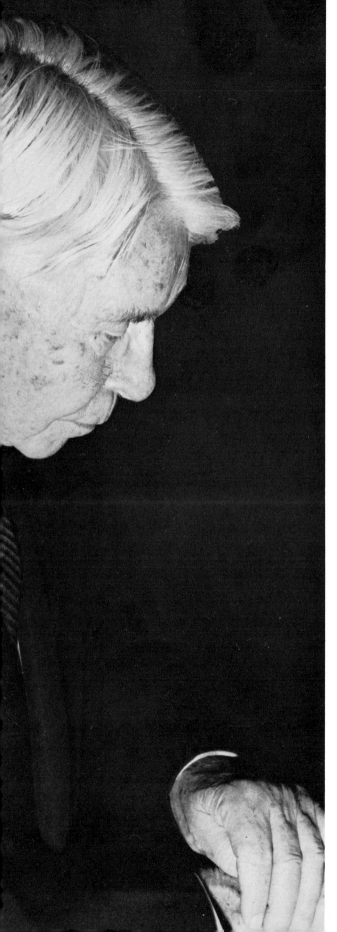

The People, Yes; *Carl Sandburg, yes!*

CARL SANDBURG

BIRTHS.

Maria Sandburg born 30 May 1875.
Charlie Sandburg born 6 January 1878
Martin Sandburg born 29 August 1880.
Emil Sandburg born 8 October 1885
Esther Mathilda born 23 May 1888
Fred Sandburg born   October 1890
Martha Sandburg born 2 April 1893

Mary —
Charlie August
Martin Godfrey
Emil Warner
Esther Mathilda
Fred William
Martha Clara

I

The Promised Land

Millions of Europe's poor fled the Continent in the mid-nineteenth century, escaping the poverty and famine, the near slavery, the suppression of their beliefs, and the endless wars for which they were always pressed into service. They arrived in the United States with little more than dreams of freedom and opportunity, and if they found no gilded streets, at least they had arrived in a vast new land unscarred by Europe's petty nationalisms, where there was room to live and where there was freedom.

When Alfred Danielsson arrived in New York City with his parents, after the long steerage voyage from Sweden in a sailing ship, it was 1856 and he was ten years old. Because the Nilssons had been a poor family in Asbo, the boy had never learned to write, and when his parents died in a widespread epidemic, Alfred's ties with his homeland were severed.

Danielsson worked in a cheese factory in Herkimer, New York. When a distant cousin, Magnus Holmes, wrote to him that "chances were all good" in Galesburg, Illinois, Danielsson crossed the land, working on railroad gangs, to the little town of 15,000 on the Illinois prairie. There, for reasons which are obscure (some have surmised that it was because there were so many Scandinavian railroad workers whose names ended in -*son*), he changed his name to August Sandburg, abandoning his Swedish patronymic, Danielsson (son of Daniel).

Carl Sandburg

Clara Mathilda Andersdotter was born on June 20, 1850, in Appuna, Sweden, and she was six when her mother died. Her father remarried, and because she was unable to get along with her step-mother, Clara emigrated to the United States at the age of twenty-three. She settled in Bushnell, Illinois, where she found work as a hotel maid and kitchen helper.

August Sandburg arrived in Bushnell as a laborer with a railroad work gang. He met Clara there, and they were married on August 7, 1874. They settled in Galesburg, where there was a growing Swedish immigrant community, and Sandburg became a blacksmith in the Chicago, Burlington and Quincy Railroad shops.

The young couple found a tiny frame cottage on Third Street, only a block from the shops, and there their first child, Mary, was born. The second of their seven children, and their first son, was born shortly after midnight on January 6, 1878. On a narrow bed with a cornhusk mattress the baby was delivered with the help of a midwife. A few days later he was baptized Charlie August Sandburg, and this name was duly recorded by Mrs. Sandburg in the family's Swedish Bible.

Although the Sandburgs were a poor family (August never earned more than 14 cents an hour for six ten-hour days of hot, hard work at the forge each week), Carl Sandburg would always remember the days of his childhood as an almost lyrical Midwestern boyhood.

If the food was simple, shoes were a luxury, and lard was wel-comed as a palatable substitute for butter, the Sandburgs never starved, and they enjoyed American luxuries such as soft white bread. There were bad years when depression afflicted the nation and August Sandburg was able to work only half time, earning $19 or $20 a month. Then Christmas meant only a little candy, an orange, and a sad, apologetic look from the father. But there were good years, too, when there was a present—perhaps a scarf or a pocket knife.

The elder Sandburg was a simple, frugal man, of whom the neighborhood grocer, Will Olson, said, "He gets to work on time, he works hard, his word is good, and you can count on him." After his long day at the forge was over, August spent his evenings doing repairs around his house or working in his little garden. Sometimes he read from his Swedish Bible, and other times he played a few chords on a small accordion, singing over and over the same old Swedish folk song.

The young couple found a tiny frame cottage on Third Street, and it was here that Carl Sandburg was born.

ABOVE August Sandburg, Carl Sandburg's father, when he worked, at the age of twenty-eight (1874), in a railroad section gang.

LEFT The room in which Charlie (Carl) Sandburg was born on January 6, 1878.

LEFT   *The South Street house —the Sandburg family's second home. They lived in it in 1881 and 1882.*

RIGHT   *The house on Berrien Street—the third home of the Sandburg family, in which they lived from 1882 to 1899.*

BELOW   *The C.B. & O. blacksmith shop where Carl Sandburg's father worked as a "helper."*

August adored his growing family, and he never tired of teasing and tossing the newest member. But his other pleasures were few. Occasionally he permitted himself the luxury of a puff or two on half of the thin cigar the grocer gave him each month when he paid his bill. (To stretch this luxury, he always cut the cigar in two with his pocket knife.) In the winter he purchased one small bottle of whiskey, which lasted until spring because August allowed himself only a teaspoonful now and then in his evening coffee.

Beyond the doors of his home, August Sandburg's interests were limited to his membership in the local Swedish Lutheran church and in the Republican Party—both symbols to him of his new status as a responsible citizen of the American democracy. But even these institutions could claim little of his time, for he had little leisure. He attended church with a fair regularity, voted Republican in elections, and attended an occasional party rally or parade.

Perhaps because he never really mastered the English language, August Sandburg was given to frequent silences and never seemed to get as close to his children as their mother did. Clara had more time for her children—to talk and to play with them. Carl Sandburg remembered that his mother had gone further in school than her husband and that it had not been difficult for her to become proficient in English. As they grew older and Swedish was spoken less and less in their home, the children found it easier to communicate with their mother than with their father, and they felt closer to her than to him.

For little Charlie Sandburg, Galesburg's dusty streets provided the background for almost a typical Midwestern boyhood of the eighties. From the afternoon school bell until it was time for supper, the boys and girls played children's games on the street. On Sundays the Sandburgs attended church and often visited the farm of their friends, the John Kranses, where Charlie and his brothers would play with little Charles Krans in the haylofts and fields.

As Charlie grew older, he and his brother Martin spent evenings helping their father with gardening and other chores around the house. And sometimes Charlie, as the oldest boy, would be taken to downtown Galesburg by his father to view such exciting events as a torchlight parade for James G. Blaine, the Republican candidate for President (defeated by Grover Cleveland).

When Charlie was seven, he and his father watched the solemn

29

Charles Krans and his wife, Emma, on their Knox County farm. As young-sters, Sandburg and Krans played in the haylofts of this barn, and many years later Sandburg wrote of "that old barn" in The People, Yes.

parade staged in Galesburg after the death of Ulysses S. Grant, and he wrote of the event in his autobiography, *Always the Young Strangers*:

> I remember how hard I tried to think about what the war was and what General Grant did that made him the greatest general of all. I went to bed that night saying I hope sometime I would know more about the war, about the black people made free, about Grant the general and what it was like to be President and the head man of the government in Washington.

To Americans at that time "the war" meant the American Civil War, and it was a popular topic of conversation in the Illinois prairie town, where men who had campaigned for Abraham Lincoln liked to reminisce of the times they had spoken with him, shaken his hand, and heard him speak, right there in Galesburg.

The Civil War was important to the people of Galesburg be-cause the town had been founded half a century before by settlers from Upper New York State—Presbyterians and Congregationalists who were ardent abolitionists. No one was permitted to join their churches until he had sworn to help eliminate slavery. In the turbulent years before the war, Galesburg was a major station of the Underground Railroad; runaway slaves were hidden in the steeple of Old First Ch▒▒▒ ▒ public square until they could be helped on the next l▒ ▒cape to Canada. The settlers had brought their love ▒ ▒t with them, and the first act of the Reverend Geor▒ ▒ Gale when he laid out the new town was to set asid▒ ▒ College (named for a hero of the Revolutionary Wa▒ ▒l Henry Knox, Secretary of War in George Wash-ing▒ ▒ By the time Sandburg had begun to grow up, the to▒ ▒ee colleges—Knox College, Lombard College, and B▒ College—and took pride in its nickname: the Athens ▒.

▒ many men in Galesburg for whom the names of Civ. ▒—Gettysburg, Antietam, First and Second Manassas—alway▒ ▒glory. One such veteran roomed with the Sandburgs when t▒ ▒tled into their third house. Joe Elser, an itinerant carpenter, enjoyed telling the Sandburg boys about the battles in which he had fought during four years as a private in the Union Army. Using stovewood and kindling as the opposing Union and Confederate forces, he reenacted these battles on the floor of his room.

Carl Sandburg's boyhood, as he was to remember it, was notable for a singular absence of unpleasantness. He attended the Fourth and Seventh Ward schools and played mumble peg, two old cat, and duck on a rock on the quiet streets and vacant lots. When he grew older, he played baseball and went swimming often in a nearby farmer's pond.

With the exception of the family Bible in English, purchased for $6.50 (nearly a week's wages), there were no books in the Sandburg home. Then, one day, a door-to-door salesman talked Mrs. Sandburg into buying a 75-cent one-volume *Cyclopedia of Important Facts of the World*, convincing her that it would benefit young Charlie. August Sandburg frowned over such extravagance, but accepted it silently. Charlie was ecstatic: "I hugged it. I sunk myself in its many facts and felt proud here was a book of our own that I didn't have to take back to the school library or the Public Library."

Not long after that, another traveling bookseller found Mrs. Sandburg an easy prey, again by stressing the educational benefits for her children. This time, for $1.50 (a sum for which the father worked

The Sandburgs attended the Second Church until 1889, when Pastor Carl A. Nyblad left the church to found Elim Lutheran Chapel. Pastor Nyblad had become involved in a scandal and the Sandburgs, believing him innocent, remained loyal by joining the chapel.

a day at the forge), she purchased *A History of the World and Its Great Events.* August Sandburg ranted for hours over such foolishness and roared, *"Gud bevara!"* (God help us!) But the book was kept, and Charlie submerged himself in it, learning about great wars and leaders and developing a taste for biography and history that never deserted him.

In school the boy was getting what his sixth-grade teacher, Lottie Goldquist, called the "reading habit." She told her pupils, "You don't know what good friends books can be till you try them, till you try many of them." Whatever effect her efforts may have had on the others, she helped make a reader of Charlie Sandburg.

Carl always remembered the books of his boyhood. He read *Napoleon and His Marshals* and *Washington and His Generals* by J. T. Headley and Thomas Knox's "Boy Travelers" series, but to these he preferred Hezekiah Butterworth's *Zigzag Journeys.* Best of all were Charles Carleton Coffin's *The Boys of '76* ("The book made me feel I could have been a boy in the days of George Washington," Sandburg wrote later); *Old Times in the Colonies* ("You were right there with those people"); and *The Story of Liberty.* But Charlie found *The Boys of '61*—Coffin's book about the Civil War—"dry and stupid," and Sandburg concluded that this was because perhaps the Civil War was "so big he couldn't get his head around it."

Of course, all the boys, "except the dumbest," read James Otis' *Toby Tyler: or, Ten Weeks with a Circus* and his *Tim and Tip: or, The Adventures of a Boy and a Dog*. Charlie read *Huckleberry Finn* and *Tom Sawyer*, too; but they did not hold the same charm for him, and he sensed that perhaps there was something in these books that was beyond a young boy, something that was for "a later time."

Through Miss Goldquist, Charlie Sandburg also discovered poetry. He was taken, as she was, with Gray's "Elegy in a Country Churchyard," and he memorized half a dozen stanzas of it—stanzas which would stay with him for three-quarters of a century. She praised Knox College alumnus Eugene Field, his "Little Boy Blue" in particular, but her favorite was Longfellow's "A Psalm of Life" ("Tell me not, in mournful numbers, / Life is but an empty dream!"), which Sandburg remembered and approved of for the "music and hope in it" all his life.

Years later Sandburg recalled how he had come to love American folk music. His father used to accompany the one Swedish song he knew on a little accordion that he chorded himself. Then August bought a little foot-pedal organ for the front room, and Mary learned to play sufficiently to accompany the family as they sang the popular songs of the period. Charlie seemed to have an inborn love of music making. He liked to hum through a pencil he held against his teeth. Soon the pencil was replaced by a comb and tissue paper, and that in turn by a kazoo, a tin fife, and a homemade cigar-box banjo. Finally, when he turned eleven and began to work, Charlie was able to save the $2 he needed to buy a secondhand banjo from Gumbiner's New York Pawn Shop. His pal Willis Calkins, whose family had come from Kentucky and still sang some of the old Anglo-Saxon ballads from that region, taught Charlie a few banjo chords for some of these songs.

Even before he was eleven, Charlie Sandburg took any errands and odd jobs that came his way to help the family's finances. When he was eleven, he was given his first regular job. Each morning at 7:45, he let himself into the second-floor office of a real estate firm, and for half an hour before he had to hurry to school, he swept the floors and emptied and cleaned the spittoons. For this, he was paid 25 cents a week. He earned an additional silver dollar a week by re-

"Olson's Corner"—much the same as it was when young Charlie Sandburg ran to the corner grocery. Next to the grocery was the butcher shop, cigar store, and shoeshop. On this corner teen-age Charlie used to hang around for hours at a time with other members of the Dirty Dozen.

porting after school to the Galesburg *Republican-Register* building to fold and deliver fifty or sixty papers a day.

One of the customers on his route was Clark E. Carr, the chubby Republican boss of Knox County. Carr had been a leader in the campaign to elect Lincoln and had been an Illinois member of the Board of Commissioners which had planned the ceremonies to dedicate the cemetery at Gettysburg. Young Charlie marveled at the fact that Carr had witnessed Abraham Lincoln's arrival at Gettysburg on horseback with "arms limp and head bent down" for that historic event.

"This roly-poly man taking the *Republican-Register* from my hand," Sandburg recalled later, "had met Lincoln in party powwows, had heard Lincoln tell stories, and Clark E. Carr said of Lincoln, 'He could make a cat laugh.'"

The boy had another customer—a wealthy man who was identified in the Galesburg city directory as a "capitalist" by trade—and the memory of this amused Sandburg when he was old enough to

34

understand it. The boy was also impressed by the young man, Fred Jeliff, who wandered through the town, notebook in hand, talking with everyone, and then returned to the *Republican-Register* offices, where he wrote the local news of the week. "I believed you could be a newspaper reporter if you could spell names and write them with a pencil on paper," Sandburg said later of his boyhood naïveté.

Charlie added to his earnings by taking on the early morning and Sunday delivery of the Chicago papers, including Victor Lawson's Chicago *Daily News*. Sandburg came to respect this paper because Lawson had insisted on the separation of news reporting from editorial bias.

When Charlie was thirteen, he was graduated from grade school, confirmed in his membership in Galesburg's Elim Lutheran Chapel, and went to work full time. The family could not afford higher education for any but their eldest child, Mary, and if she were to finish high school and go to college, Charlie would have to help buy the proper clothes and books she would need. And so, very early, his childhood was at an end.

Charlie Sandburg attended seventh and eighth grades at the Churchill School and was graduated in December, 1891.

2

In the Alger Mode

By the time he was thirteen, young Sandburg had been molded by most of the important influences that were to shape his career. There was, first, the boyhood in an Illinois prairie town during a time when Lincoln was remembered as a man of flesh and blood and where veterans of "the war" kept its events and meanings fresh. There was Charlie's discovery of the riches of books, of poetry, and of folk music. And there was his hunger for history, for a better understanding of the world and its governance, which was whetted by the one-volume histories his mother had bought, by the books he had read in school, and by the Cigarette Biographies of famous people that he had begun to collect. Charlie got the coupons for these biographies from older, smoking acquaintances, and they were as treasured by boys of his era as football cards are by boys of today.

A few more years were to pass before his urge for experience beyond that which Galesburg could provide was to send him, a vagabond, into the land. In these remaining years Galesburg brought further important influences to him.

After he had been graduated from elementary school, Charlie's full-time job was as a milkman for a man who appears in Sandburg's autobiography under the name of George Burton. The boy worked seven days a week, lugging two milkcans along his route to fill the pitchers and cans brought out to him by housewives, and for this, he was paid $12 a month. He kept the job as long as he was able to endure the embittered Burton, who begrudged the boy the time he had to stay home, first because of illness and later because of a family tragedy.

In October, 1892, Charlie and his brother Martin were ill for a few days, apparently only with sore throats. Then the two younger boys—Emil, going on seven, and Freddie, only two—were stricken, and when their conditions failed to improve, the costly services of a physician were finally summoned. The diagnosis was diphtheria—a terrible killer at the time—and the doctor told the distraught parents that they could only hope and pray for the boys' recovery.

But Emil and Freddie died, and years later Sandburg remembered how he and Mart tried to conceal their grief when friends visited the house to offer condolences. And, as at his grade school graduation, Sandburg did not have the proper clothes to wear to the double funeral. Mourning clothes are a luxury the poor cannot always afford.

"Freddie hadn't lived long enough to get any tangles in my heart," Sandburg recalled in later years. "But Emil I missed then, and for years I missed him and had my wonderings about what a chum and younger brother he would have made. I can see now the beaming smile from a large mouth. There have been times I imagined him saying to me, 'Life is good and why not death?' "

Confirmation class of 1891, Elim Lutheran Chapel, Galesburg, Illinois. Front row (left to right): Carl Sandburg, John Johnson, Rev. Carl A. Nyblad, Fred O. Johnson. Back row (left to right): J. Robert Ebberstein, Emil Nelson, Axel Johnson, Herman Johnson, Oscar F. "Husky" Larson.

Carl Sandburg

After the funeral Sandburg told Burton that he was quitting the job. "Well, I guess that'll be no loss to me," the soured man said. Yet young Sandburg could not despise Burton because he pitied the older man so much for his joyless life.

For the next few years Sandburg tried his hand at whatever jobs came his way. He was a chore boy in a drugstore, he shined shoes as a porter in a downtown barbershop, and he worked as a bottle-washer, a potter's helper, and a stagehand.

During these years Charlie came into contact with people who greatly influenced his life at a later time. There was the dapper bearded man, slight and spectacled, who passed the Sandburg home each morning so regularly that the Sandburgs came to know it was eight o'clock when he walked by. He carried a tan valise in his hand and was always deep in thought. Years later Carl was to become a student of Professor Philip Green Wright at Lombard College, and many years after that, Sandburg still wondered at the strange coincidence which had brought them so close before it actually brought them together. "As a boy I didn't have the faintest dim gleam of a dream that this professor would in less than ten years become for me a fine and dear friend, a deeply beloved teacher," Sandburg wrote later.

Left: Carl Sandburg at the age of fourteen was working as a milk delivery boy after his graduation from grammar school. Center: Charles August Sandburg at the age of twenty when he had returned from Puerto Rico and was about to enter Lombard College. Right: Martin G. Sandburg at the age of eleven.

The old Union Hotel building in the Public Square still stands. Here Carl Sandburg shined shoes and worked as a porter in Humphrey's Barber shop from November, 1893, to the early part of 1895.

At this point Sandburg feared that his formal schooling had come to an end. He did not begrudge turning over a portion of his wages to his parents to help put his sister Mary through school, but he had a deep hunger for more learning. To nourish it, he read omnivorously whatever was at hand—almanacs, the pharmaceutical books at the drugstore, volumes from the public library, and Mary's textbooks. Finding the Latin and mathematics texts too difficult to study without tutelage, he concentrated on Mary's literature courses and read almost all the assigned novels by the popular Irving, Scott, and Hawthorne. The characters in *The Scarlet Letter* troubled him by the injustice of their Puritanism. Galesburg, small town that it was, still had its town drunks and its broken marriages, a rare crime of violence, a brothel, and a few prostitutes, and the older boys were aware of this side of Galesburg life. Charlie Sandburg, at least, came to accept such things as realities and valid, if unpleasant, facets of life. The only intolerance he ever seemed to develop was of intolerant people.

In these years when Sandburg was being forced to mature rather early, the Sjodin family moved to Galesburg from Chicago. Mr. Sjodin was a journeyman tailor, whose political sentiments ran to anarchism, Populism, and Socialism—highly radical notions for that era. Sandburg

39

was to remember him as a man whose walk seemed to proclaim, "I cringe before no man."

The tailor's son, John, who was two or three years older than Charlie Sandburg, became his closest friend. In Charlie, John found an eager listener for the "hard-and-fast political-action radical" notions he had learned from his father. "There are companionships in early life having color and mystery," Sandburg wrote half a century later. "We cannot measure or analyze exactly what they did to us. And we like to look back on them. John Sjodin is one of these."

In their long walks in the evenings and on Sundays, John Sjodin preached doctrines that forced Charlie's mind to stretch far beyond the Lutheran-Republican limits of his family experience. The big corporations, the banks, and the railroads were the oppressors of the workingman and the farmer, Sjodin said, and the Republican and Democratic parties were their handmaidens, no matter how much these parties professed to differ at election times. But Socialism was coming, the older boy predicted, and the day was not far away when the factory workers and the farmers would organize and, in this great union, find the strength to overthrow the robber barons.

Charlie Sandburg was an eager pupil, and he began to carry home these dangerous notions and to worry his father with them at supper. The Sjodin boy was spurring young Sandburg to independent thought. "He made me know I ought to know more about what was going on in politics, industry, business, and crime over the widespread American scene."

Despite his limited leisure in these busy years, Sandburg found time for baseball with the teen-age boys of the town and for a dip, in hot weather, at local swimming holes. One weekend he and a friend took a train trip—Sandburg's first—to the state fair at Peoria. He began to attend dances and, shyly, to meet the pretty girls of the town. He found himself so bashful that he was unable to utter the tender thoughts that came to his mind about the girls' beauty and grace.

Sometimes, when he was in his middle teens, he and some other boys got involved in peccadilloes which caused their parents to shake their heads and worry over the fate of the younger generation. They used to gather during the evening on a corner under the new electric streetlights, where they talked and sang and laughed so loudly that the neighbors called the police, who came to scold the boys. They annoyed unfriendly neighbors by tossing strings of tin cans onto their

Galesburg's "Finest" caught Carl Sandburg and other members of Dirty Dozen swimming naked in the Old Brick swimming hole. The gang had to spend a night in the Cherry Street calaboose.

porches, while the young scamps hid nearby in the darkness to enjoy the commotion.

But the worst crime these scalawags committed was enacted on the day they went swimming in the nude in a mudhole near the edge of town. Some shocked neighbors called the police. The police rounded up the boys, Sandburg among them, and hauled them to the local jail, "a hot stuffy place," where they were held overnight. "We had been boys at play, swimming for the pure joy of it, but the law had been broken and we had to suffer for it. That sort of thing makes a boy wonder about himself and what laws are good for." The next morning they were lectured by a justice of the peace and then freed. The incident seems hardly worth serious discussion, but Sandburg recalled it bitterly for years and permitted it to color his attitude

41

toward all powers that be. Years later Sandburg remarked to his friend Harry Hansen about it, "There were times when I might easily have stepped over the line that marks the honest man from the law-breaker. I mean conditions often drive a man to hate the law."

In 1895, when Charlie was seventeen, he went to work as a milkman again—this time for Samuel Kossuth Barlow, who was an entirely different kind of man from Burton, and Sandburg came to love and respect him. Barlow had been a country dance fiddler before he became a dairyman, and he still liked to get out his fiddle and play through such reels and hoedowns as "Money Musk," "Mrs. Macleod's Reel" and "Pop Goes the Weasel." Barlow was a happy man, who relished life and loved his wife, his business, his town, his friends, and women in general, whom he treated courteously. His good-natured stoicism appealed to Sandburg.

When Charlie aired his radical new sentiments for Barlow, preaching to him about the wrongs the rich were committing against the poor and hinting darkly about the terrible day of reckoning that was coming, Barlow stumped the boy by replying playfully, "There's just getting to be too many people in the world. . . . We've got to have a war and kill off a lot of 'em before times will get real better."

Each morning for the sixteen months he carried milk for Barlow, Sandburg crossed the Knox College campus on his way to Barlow's dairy. And each day Sandburg walked past the college's Old Main Building, where a bronze plaque had been placed to commemorate the fourth Lincoln-Douglas debate, which had been held there before a crowd of 20,000 on October 7, 1858. This confrontation between the opposing senatorial candidates in the national election of 1858 was the one in which Lincoln recognized that slavery was the crucial issue upon which he would stake his political career. Each time he passed Old Main, "in winter sunrise, in broad summer daylight, in falling snow or rain, in all weathers of the year," Sandburg read the quotation from Lincoln's speech and committed it to memory: "He is blowing out the moral lights around us, when he contends that who-ever wants slaves has a right to hold them."

While riding the milk wagon along his route, Sandburg often read—sometimes aloud—William Jennings Bryan's "Cross of Gold" speech and Thomas E. Watson's *The People's Party Campaign Book*. (Watson was an early Populist leader, who, years later in Georgia, where he was elected to the U. S. Senate, became a notorious racist

ABOVE *Every morning on the way to his job as a milkman, Sandburg passed the east front of Knox College's Old Main Building, where Lincoln and Douglas had debated in October, 1858.*

BELOW *At the north front of Old Main, Sandburg paused to read the words of Abraham Lincoln, and these words always stayed with him.*

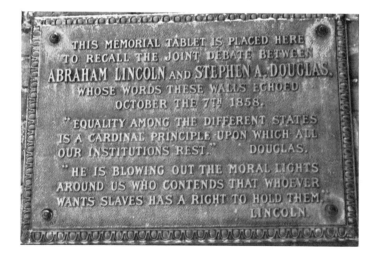

THIS MEMORIAL TABLET IS PLACED HERE
TO RECALL THE JOINT DEBATE BETWEEN
ABRAHAM LINCOLN AND STEPHEN A. DOUGLAS,
WHOSE WORDS THESE WALLS ECHOED
OCTOBER THE 7TH 1858.

"EQUALITY AMONG THE DIFFERENT STATES
IS A CARDINAL PRINCIPLE UPON WHICH ALL
OUR INSTITUTIONS REST."   DOUGLAS.

"HE IS BLOWING OUT THE MORAL LIGHTS
AROUND US WHO CONTENDS THAT WHOEVER
WANTS SLAVES HAS A RIGHT TO HOLD THEM."
LINCOLN.

and anti-Semite.) And Sandburg recited Gray's "Elegy" and writings and speeches of the controversial freethinker Robert Ingersoll. He especially appreciated Ingersoll's eulogy on the death of his brother, Eben, a Congressman: "Life is a narrow vale between the cold and barren peaks of two eternities. . . . We cry aloud—and the only answer is the echo of our wailing cry. . . . Were every one to whom he did some loving service to bring a blossom to his grave, he would sleep tonight beneath a wilderness of flowers."

Each of these men was a hero to Sandburg. Another was John Peter Altgeld, governor of Illinois. When Altgeld was campaigning for election in 1892, Sandburg heard the lean, bearded, cold-eyed man orate for ninety minutes without passion and without altering his stance. A few months after his election, Altgeld obeyed his conscience and pardoned the three surviving anarchists who had been convicted in the slaying of seven policemen in the Haymarket Square riot of 1886. Altgeld reasoned—and time has proved him correct—that there was no real evidence that these men had been involved in the bombing of the policemen who had come to break up an anarchist meeting. They had been found guilty, Altgeld concluded, only as a result of the hatred of, fear of, and prejudice against anarchism prevalent at the time.

Sandburg devoted two hours to reading Altgeld's long, well-reasoned statement about his decision, and the boy remembered how he had dumbly agreed with the mob six years before, when he had been only a child of eight. The mob had demanded that all the accused anarchists be lynched. Altgeld, of course, destroyed his political career by his unpopular action, but he gained the lasting admiration of all decent men, among them Carl Sandburg.

On the Knox campus Sandburg often passed an elderly slight man, who always nodded in greeting. Newton Bateman was then a Knox professor and a former president of the college, but in the 1850's he had been state superintendent of public instruction in Springfield. His offices in the statehouse had been next to those of Lincoln, when Lincoln had been a candidate for President. Once, Bateman liked to recall in later years, Lincoln had brought him a letter to correct, confessing, "I never was very strong on grammar." And Bateman remembered seeing Lincoln pacing in his office, worried over the growing inevitability of civil war, and saying, "I am nothing but the truth is everything." In 1860, when Lincoln boarded the train in Springfield for his inauguration in Washington, the last man to shake hands with him was Bateman.

In addition to the Lincoln associations, Knox played several important roles in Sandburg's teen-age life. Probably because he was unable to pursue his education, Sandburg thirsted for culture and knowledge and attended whatever public events he was able to at Knox—lectures and debates, music recitals and speech contests, and even graduation exercises.

In 1896, when John Huston Finley, president of Knox College, organized a celebration to mark the thirty-eighth anniversary of the Lincoln-Douglas debate on the campus, Sandburg took time from his milk route to attend. Among the speakers were Chauncey M. Depew, president of the New York Central Railroad, who had stumped for Lincoln in 1864, and Senator John M. Palmer, who had helped found the Republican Party in 1856 and had served as a delegate to its convention four years later in Chicago, where he supported Lincoln's bid for the Presidential nomination.

Another guest was Robert Todd Lincoln, then a wealthy Chicago corporation lawyer. Sandburg studied him and wondered about the memories that he had of his life and conversations with his father in the White House. And Sandburg thought about what Abraham Lincoln had stood for and how paradoxical it was that his only suriviving son had represented the Pullman Company against the workers in the bloody Chicago strike of 1894.

Earlier that year, in June, Charlie Sandburg made his first trip to the "big city," which, to the people of Galesburg, meant Chicago. He talked his father into getting him a free C.B. & Q. pass for the round trip, and with $1.50 and no luggage, he rode the Burlington at last toward Chicago.

He arrived at Chicago's Union Station, wearing his rough clothes and his old fisherman's hat. His first glimpse was of Canal Street, with horses everywhere pulling drays, buggies, and delivery wagons through swirling dust, their hoofbeats adding a staccato rhythm to the din of street construction.

Hiking east across the Adams Street bridge, he began his three-day walking tour of the city. Each day began with wheatcakes and coffee at Pittsburgh Joe's, a cheap diner at Van Buren and Clark streets, where he also ate dinner and supper at a dime a meal. Lodging on South State Street cost him 25 cents a night for a shabby sleeping

Chicago's Union Depot, where eighteen-year-old Sandburg arrived on the No. 12 Express at 2:05 P.M. on June 15, 1896.

room, but that did not trouble him. He was finally seeing Chicago, and he was on the longest trip he had ever made away from home.

All his waking hours (and he was up early and into bed late) he spent trudging through the city. He goggled at the elevated tracks under construction that would encircle the heart of downtown and give it its nickname, the Loop. He visited the fabled department stores, Marshall Field's and Carson Pirie Scott & Company, and he walked past the plant of the Chicago *Daily News.* Only a few years before he had delivered its papers, and in another twenty years he was to become one of its most famous staff members.

Sandburg was aware, with his recently awakened social instincts, of the inequities he saw in this raw, bustling city. For it was really two cities: the city of the merchant and industrial princes, the Fields and Armours and Pullmans and Palmers; and the city of everyone else— the lowliest stockyard and factory workers and the shopgirls and clerks

46

ABOVE *He goggled at the elevated tracks under construction.*

BELOW *He visited the fabled department stores—Marshall Field's and Carson Pirie Scott & Company.*

at the bottom of the ladder. It was a city ripe for the exposure it was to experience at the pens of Dreiser and Upton Sinclair, Lincoln Steffens and, some years later, Sandburg himself.

Wandering as far east as the city would permit, he came to Lake Michigan and its vista of endless horizon made an impression he was never to forget. Sixty years later he wrote of that first meeting: "Those born to it don't know what it is for a boy to hear about it for years and then comes a day when for the first time he sees water stretching away before his eyes and running to meet the sky."

He saw vaudeville shows and a wax museum, and he visited the Board of Trade, where men gambled with the farmers' futures. He sought out the Des Plaines Street police station, from which officers had marched to Haymarket Square that tragic day a decade before, and he marched their route to the scene of the bombing.

Perhaps he saw Chicago's painted women under the street lights, as he was to write some years later, to the dismay of many critics of poetry. Or maybe his experience with these women on that first trip was the one he related years later. He had stopped for the free lunch in a saloon, and a young woman with "hard lines at the mouth and eyes" smiled a "hard smile" and asked him, "Lookin' fer a good time?" He wisecracked, and she flared angrily at him. Then he said apologetically, "You're up the wrong alley, sister. I ain't got but two nickels and they wouldn't do you any good." She rose, bid him a cheerful farewell, and sought her fortune at another table.

"I rode home to Galesburg," he remembered, "and tried to tell the folks what Chicago was like." A few years earlier poverty had forced him to abandon childhood. Now, perhaps, with his first visit to the big city he had begun to lose his small-town naïveté.

When his sister Mary was graduated, Charlie spent some of his hard-earned money to help buy her white graduation dress, and he also bought her a dozen red roses. Mary was going to be a grade school teacher, and Charlie confided to her, "I'm going away. I'm going to be a writer. And if I find I can't be a writer, I'll be a hobo."

If Mary was surprised by his confession, it can have been only because she was not aware of the restlessness and perplexity which had been troubling her younger brother in those years. He was tormented by questions which probably had never disturbed his parents:

OPPOSITE *He saw vaudeville shows and a wax museum.*

Skyscrapers of the "Windy City," as Carl Sandburg first saw them.

What was the purpose of life? What was the meaning of America? Why had Charlie Sandburg been born? These enigmas drove him into fits of depression in which, he later confessed, suicide was contemplated. Somehow he fought against such a solution until this notion came to him: "If death is what you want all you have to do is to live on and it will come to you like a nice surprise you never imagined." He opted to live.

But he had come to scorn his hometown, his people, and himself. It was hard to understand, but he finally realized that the trouble lay within himself. He wanted something Galesburg was unable to give him. He did not know yet what it was, but he yearned to leave his home to search for it. Somewhere out there, he sensed, he might find himself, learn who he was and what he was meant to do.

"Now I would take to The Road," he wrote in later years, "see rivers and mountains, every day meeting strangers to whom I was one more young stranger."

3

On the Road

CHARLIE SANDBURG was restless during the year 1897. The slight muscular youth had attained his full growth of five feet ten inches, and at nineteen, his manhood was upon him. And what had he accomplished? The best steady job he had held was as a milkman, and that had led to a dead end. His formal education was over, he believed. In his life so far, he had journeyed away from Galesburg only four times—to a convention of his church's youth league, to the Illinois River on a camping trip, to the state fair at Peoria, and to Chicago. And because he was shy and "couldn't think of what to say till after I left them, and then wasn't sure," he had no girl.

Life was empty and meaningless. So the young man decided to take to the road as a hobo. He wanted to ride the freights west into Kansas, to seek work in the wheat harvests, and to "see what happened."

He was away from home four months on that first jaunt, and it was a daring adventure for a small-town boy who had never been away for more than three days before. It was the last week in June when Sandburg ran alongside a moving Santa Fe freight train heading west and leaped through the wide doorway of a boxcar. His baggage was in his pockets: pocket knife, needles and thread, soap, comb, razor, pocket mirror, two handkerchiefs, pipe and tobacco, a watch, and $3.25, his life's savings.

Carl Sandburg

Standing in the open doorway, he watched the ranks of green corn march past and read the station names of strange towns. As he crossed the long railroad bridge over the Mississippi, the sight of the mighty river began to assuage the gnawing wanderlust. It was the border then, separating the settled Middle West from the frontier lands. He leaped from the train at Fort Madison, Iowa, into the rain and bought a nickel's worth of cheese and crackers, glorying in his first venture out of Illinois. He worked passage on a steamboat, loading and unloading kegs of nails, to Keokuk, where he met a hobo who offered to share one of his "lumps" (a package of buttered bread and slices of roast beef) with Charlie. He accepted and then regretted the acquaintance when the new friend sought to put a hand on Charlie in a suspicious way. Sandburg walked off, alone again.

That was how his great adventure started: the lift of new lands, darkened by a shadow of the unspeakable. But the novelty of freedom was stronger than the smudge of unpleasant reality. After all, Charlie had known about the prostitutes of Galesburg. He had listened to the Civil War veterans speak about the joys of women, and he had been solicited in Chicago. He was a man of the world.

He wandered on—to wait on tables in a lunch counter in Keokuk; to work on a railroad section gang at Bean Lake, Missouri, until the steady diet of fried potatoes and pork sickened him; to vend hot tamales on the streets of Kansas City; to pitch wheat in Pawnee County, Kansas; and to labor in the dust with the threshing crews in the harvest. In Denver, the farthest west he hoboed that trip, he washed dishes in a restaurant and marveled at the grandeur of the Rocky Mountains.

Throughout his wandering Sandburg kept a log of his adventures in two small notebooks. In them he recorded word impressions of the land, and he experimented with the textures and potentials of language. He jotted down the lyrics of the songs he learned from rivermen and stevedores, farmhands and hoboes, cowboys and railroadmen.

Dramatic adventures were few, but he never forgot them. A bandit who preyed on the harvest workers tried to interest young Sandburg in a life of crime. A "shack" (a railroad brakeman) extorted a quarter from him, threatening to toss the youth from a moving gondola car if he did not pay. He met other "gaycats," as the hoboes romantically called themselves, in the hobo jungles, where they swapped victuals and coffee, yarns and songs. In Lindsborg, Kansas, he worked for

52

the Swedish settlers in the harvest, and he was allowed to sleep in a barn. One morning he heard one of his kinsmen shout out, referring to him, "Is that bum up yet?" and his feelings were hurt.

He listened carefully to the people's speech, their slang and their sayings, and he began to collect examples of folk wisdom.

By October he was back in Galesburg at "the only house in the United States where I could open a door without knocking and walk in for a kiss from the woman of the house." He exhibited his profit—$15 and some cents—but he was unable to show his family the meaningful effects of the trip. When he had left Galesburg, he had been a reticent young man, uncertain of who or what he was. Now, as he put it, he had learned to stand on his own feet, to look people in the eye, to speak freely with ready answers for any unexpected questions, and he later wrote of his return, "Away deep in my heart now I had hope as never before. Struggles lay ahead, I was sure, but whatever they were I would not be afraid of them."

Back in Galesburg, he sought to learn a trade, to begin to make something of himself. He became a house painter's apprentice, a job that entailed climbing up and down ladders, carrying supplies, and sanding walls so the older men could paint them. But the apprentice

Going to war.

was not permitted to paint any houses, and Sandburg grew impatient again.

Then the battleship *Maine* was sunk in Havana Harbor, and the United States went to war with Spain. When Company C, Sixth Illinois Regiment, was formed in Galesburg early in 1898, Sandburg was one of the first men to enlist. He traveled with the militia company to Springfield, where it was mustered in, and after ten days of drilling in civvies, the new soldiers were issued their gear, which included the same dark-blue uniforms that Union privates had worn in the Civil War. In his off-duty time Sandburg roamed the state capital and visited, for the first time, the former home of Abraham Lincoln. It was the first house the Lincolns had owned.

Then his regiment was entrained for Falls Church, Virginia, (seven miles outside Washington), and Charlie Sandburg had the opportunity to visit the Capitol, where Congress was in session, and to walk past the White House and wonder what President McKinley was doing. He visited Ford's Theater and the Peterson House across the street, where Lincoln had died. Inspired, he recited to a soldier buddy a verse from one of Lincoln's favorite poems, by William Knox, beginning:

> Oh why should the spirit of mortal be proud?
> Like a fast-flitting meteor, a fast-flying cloud,
> A flash of the lightning, a break of the wave,
> He passed from life to his rest in the grave.

They embarked on the freighter *Rita*, and when they arrived in Cuba, they found the situation well in hand. So, without leaving the ship, the regiment cruised on to Puerto Rico. Sandburg and his comrades saw no action on the island, but they marched across it in tropical heat, rain, and muck, amid mosquitoes big enough to kill a dog (or so they bragged), and Sandburg suffered a running battle with dysentery, its miseries compounded by the tasteless rations of tinned beef, beans, and bean soup. But serious now about his desire to write, he managed to dash off long letters to the Galesburg *Daily Mail* and acted as its authentic, volunteer, part-time war correspondent in Puerto Rico.

After five months he was back in Galesburg with $122 in mustering-out pay. It had not been much of a war, but as Sandburg was to state correctly later, it did launch the United States as a world power.

TOP LEFT   *Carl Sandburg's Army discharge papers from the Spanish-American War.*

TOP RIGHT   *In 1899 Charles A. Sandburg earned his tuition at Lombard College by tolling this bell atop the Old Main.*

BOTTOM   *Company C, Sixth Illinois Regiment, home from the war.*

Now he was twenty, with his war behind him. He had hoboed west to the Rockies and soldiered east to tropical islands.

His brother Mart asked him, "Well, last year you were a hobo and this year a soldier; so what's next with you?"

"Maybe I'll go to college," said Charles A. Sandburg, and it was under this impressive name that he registered at Lombard College where he was accepted as a provisional student—provisional because he had not attended high school. Charles was able to take this step because, as a veteran, he was entitled to free tuition at Lombard—a smaller school than Knox, with only 12 instructors and 125 students, but a considerably more liberal one as a result of its affiliation with the freethinking Universalist Church.

Mart asked the mayor to find Charlie a city job so that he could work his way through school, and he was hired as call man for the local fire department at $10 a month. Charlie Sandburg slept in the station at night, and when there was a fire, he slid down the brass pole to sound the alarm. Then, on bicycle if necessary, he rounded up the sleeping fire fighters. He also took a job as bellringer at Lombard. He had to climb the college tower to signal the end and beginning of classes. While waiting in the tower for class times, he read through the stacks of Universalist tracts which were stored there. The tracts provided another seed of the agnosticism that was to supplant Lutheranism in his mature years.

Charlie's decision to accept the opportunity to attend college made his mother and father very proud. They were beginning to see their children enjoy the opportunities they had sought by emigrating to the United States. "You do the best you can, Charlie," his mother told him, "and maybe make a name for yourself. It don't do any hurt to try."

4

A Great Teacher

His enrollment at Lombard brought Charles Sandburg under one of the decisive influences of his life. For the next decade, for several years of it through daily contact, he became first a disciple and then an intimate friend of Philip Green Wright—one of those rare scholars who cherish an authentic reverence for knowledge and the arts and possess an ability to impart it to their students.

Sandburg elected to study English, Latin, speech, and inorganic chemistry. He was an earnest student, who not only earned good grades but found time as well for a full schedule of extracurricular activities. He plunged into about as much collegiate life as the little campus offered. In his four years at Lombard he captained a winning basketball team; sang with the glee club; served as business manager of the *Lombard Review;* won the school checkers championship; debated for the Erosophian Society (after a nervous start he went on to win $15 in gold coins in the spring of 1901 for an oration on John Ruskin that the *Review* published under the title "A Man with Ideals"), served as coeditor of *The Cannibal: Jubilee Year Book* in 1901; and was editor in chief of the *Review* in his senior year.

The young man also managed to find time to establish, with some of his old pals of the Dirty Dozen (the nickname of a group of teenaged boys he had played with), the Monarch dancing club in response to the formation of another organization, the Crescent Club, by some other young men. The clubs sponsored dances on alternate weekends, renting a hall at a cost of 25 cents a member, and hiring the Hoyles Family Orchestra (father, son, and two daughters) for these affairs. Sometimes, between dances, Cully, as his friends then called Sandburg, strummed a guitar and sang popular ballads of the period, as well as some of the less earthy folk songs he had learned on the road.

A confident young man now, Sandburg waltzed and two-stepped with most of the pretty girls in town. Sometimes he walked one of them to her home, although he still had trouble finding the right words. In his old age he was to remember the young women of Galesburg as "lovely girls who could have gone anywhere and held their own for looks, manners, and smooth dancing." A few of them, in particular, he was never to forget. One was Alice Harshberger, whom he called Allie, who had looks that "would have been welcome by any painter seeking a model."

Many years later, in her eighties and the widow of Wilson Henderson, Allie remembered that Cully had always asked her to save a waltz for him and that, although he was shy, he had been a good dancer. She also recalled how she had lured Sandburg's interest away from another girl by reminding him that her rival harbored strong Republican sentiments that completely opposed Sandburg's liberal beliefs.

To finance all his interests, Sandburg took on as many jobs as he could find. In addition to serving as call man for the fire department and bellringer for the school, he became janitor for the college gymnasium and a salesman of stereoscopic views in Galesburg and the surrounding farmlands. To all his endeavors, he gave his substantial energy.

Occasionally, enthusiasm was not sufficient to enable him to prevail. In May, 1899, Representative George W. Prince of Illinois notified the officers of C Company of the Sixth Illinois Regiment that one of its veterans was entitled to an appointment to the U. S. Military Academy at West Point. The officers conferred and selected Sandburg to take the test—a tribute to the impression he had made on them in his short Army service in the rank of private. Sandburg journeyed to the Army academy and took its entrance examinations, and for two weeks until the results were posted, he was a classmate of Douglas MacArthur and Ulysses S. Grant III. But Sandburg's lack of the rudiments of secondary education was his undoing. He failed the examination in mathematics and in grammar. He returned to Galesburg.

TOP LEFT *Professor Philip Green Wright influenced Carl's early manhood more than any other person, and he has been called Sandburg's literary father. Wright was a small man but a great believer in the benefits of physical culture, and he loved to ride tandem bicycles with his wife.*

TOP RIGHT *Charles August Sandburg, coeditor of* The Cannibal, *at the age of twenty-three, 1901.*

BOTTOM LEFT *Alice "Allie" Harshberger, age seventeen, saved a last waltz for "Cully" Sandburg.*

BOTTOM RIGHT *Allie Harshberger, age eighty-one, recalls fond memories of Cully Sandburg. She holds an article she wrote on "The Little-Known Mrs. Carl Sandburg."*

Carl Sandburg

In later years, with hindsight, he was to realize that this was one of the fortunate failures of his life, for it brought him within the milieu of Professor Wright.

In that time and place, on that small faculty, Wright seemed to his worshipful students to be a latter-day Leonardo. Wright was a disciple of William Morris, the English poet and designer who had died in 1896, at sixty-four, and who had sought to promote the image of the well-rounded man. Morris, in addition to writing poetry, had been interested in medieval arts and crafts, helped spur the Gothic Revival, founded the famed Kelmscott Press, for which he had designed and printed lovely books, and had written utopian romances.

Professor Wright was also a many-faceted achiever. In addition to teaching English, economics, mathematics, and astronomy, he found time to write poetry, essays, and other examples of belles lettres, which he printed on a Gordon handpress in the basement of his home. He set the type, designed covers, and created page illuminations and cover art for his books. In addition, he was a student of social history, music, art, and philosophy and a graduate civil engineer, who helped construct a bridge over the Mississippi before he turned to teaching.

In an era of social reform, Wright was a complete liberal, totally in sympathy with the efforts of labor and farmers to organize into unions and cooperatives. But he went beyond that, and he sought to understand the revolutionary writings of Marx and Engels and the doctrines of Populism, Socialism, anarchism, and Communism. By the time Sandburg became one of his students, Wright, dedicated to humanism, had become a member of the Socialist Party.

This was the time, too, when there was born a renewed interest in Lincoln—not as the godhead who had held the republic together through its most terrible challenge, but as the man who had struggled against his own weaknesses to do what he thought was right. Wright was very much aware of this growing study. When he was at Harvard as a graduate student in 1886 and 1887, the Nicolay-Hay "official" biography of Lincoln was serialized in *Century* Magazine. In 1894, Wright's second year at Lombard, the same authors published their two-volume *Complete Works of Abraham Lincoln,* and the following year *McClure's Magazine* printed Ida M. Tarbell's study of Lincoln as a man beset by doubts of his abilities to cope with the awesome responsibilities of his office. When Sandburg was Wright's student, the professor often discussed this emerging human view of Lincoln.

Professor Wright's liberalism found an eager response in Sandburg. The young man remembered the lean days of his childhood, when workmen such as his father were at the mercy of nationwide economic fluctuations and when he had been an avid listener to the Socialistic talk of John Sjodin. Sandburg's vision of democracy was shaped, too, by the early liberalism of Bryan, by the courageous championship of social justice for which Altgeld had sacrificed his career, and, of course, by his admiration of Lincoln.

Later, trying to explain how he had arrived at his own interpretation of Lincoln, Sandburg told a biographer, Karl Detzer, "I do remember, though, that when I was in college at Galesburg I resolved that some day I would go farther in the study of Lincoln, in the hope of getting a better understanding of this man the Republican party and the G. A. R. and the preachers magnified until he was too big to see."

Under Wright's influence, Sandburg studied John Ruskin, Walter Pater, Leo Tolstoy, and even Elbert Hubbard, the "sage of East Aurora (New York)," whose monthly magazine *Little Journeys* offered such homely advice as "If you work for a man, in heaven's name work for him!" and "The final proof of greatness lies in being able to endure contumely without resentment." Sandburg also began to read, for Wright's classes, such writers as Carlyle, Emerson, Kipling, Browning, Irving, Addison, and, of course, Shakespeare. In this period Sandburg bought a secondhand copy, for 10 cents, of Charles Lamb's *Last Essays of Elia*, which he was to treasure throughout his life.

These were good years for Sandburg, and he began finally to realize who he was and what he wanted to do with his life. If the realization came later to him than to other young people, just as much of his recognition was to come later in life for him, it was with no diminution of richness. He was now writing for school publications and experimenting with prose and poetry for himself. He was a prizewinning speaker, an athlete, and a serious scholar. He was, in short, a big man on that small campus. And he fell in love a few times in those days, "but not too deep."

Professor Wright, that man of many talents, wrote a musical play, *The Cannibal Converts*, which was staged by the students of Lombard University (the school was renamed in 1900) in the Galesburg Opera House. The play was about a group of Lombard students who were kicked in a giant football toward the Philippines but who landed by mistake on a cannibal island. Who was the cannibal chief waiting with

TOP LEFT *Oscar F. "Husky" Larson, age sixteen, when he and Sandburg were members of the Dirty Dozen gang.*

TOP RIGHT *Husky Larson in 1963, age eighty-five, remembers his rivalry with Cully Sandburg for the attentions of Allie Harshberger.*

BOTTOM *Captain of Lombard's basketball team, Sandburg holds the ball.*

lampblacked skin to menace them in unintelligible gibberish? It was Carl Sandburg, who was finally persuaded to abandon his primitive state and to travel to Lombard, where he would become civilized.

About this time Sandburg got a job writing promotional copy for a traveling "magnetic healer," J. Austin Larsen. One of his bonus ideas for Larsen was a suggestion that the confidence man spell out his name on stage with the crutches of the cripples he had supposedly cured with his magic touch. "If and when I meet St. Peter at the gate," Sandburg told a good friend of his later years, author Harry Golden, "I wouldn't be surprised if he said, 'What about your work with J. Austin Larsen back in Anno Domini 1901? Do you think you belong up here or down there?' "

Years later Wright's son Quincy, who later became a respected professor of international law at the University of Chicago, remembered Sandburg's visits to the Wright home in Galesburg: "Carl was frequently around our house, talking with father about Walt Whitman and other subjects in the field of Literature. They also discoursed on such subjects as economic reform and socialism. Carl's interest did not extend into mathematics as I recall it, though I think he sometimes looked at the stars through our telescope."

Another of Wright's students of those years, Athol Brown, later remarked of the teacher: "He seemingly only sought to stir us into action in order to see what would happen." With Sandburg, the technique was effective, and the role Wright played cannot be overstated. Sandburg was beginning to write in earnest now. He, Brown, and a few other students were among a select handful who were regularly invited to Wright's house to discuss literature. As Quincy Wright remembered these evenings, "They read aloud from Kipling, Turgenev and Mark Twain, to suit all tastes. [Sandburg] also belonged to the 'Poor Writers Club,' a more select group of four or five budding literary artists that met with father to read to one another their own productions."

In addition to criticizing one another's work, they discussed politics, social reform, and the important issues of the day. At one point, Wright and Sandburg read and analyzed in depth Karl Marx's *Das Kapital,* which was not to become a controversial subject on many larger and supposedly more progressive campuses for some decades to come.

With his success in college and with the stimulating guidance he received, it is puzzling that Charles Sandburg suddenly left Lombard in 1902, only a few months before graduation, without obtaining his degree. His family tried to talk him out of it. Mary was now a teacher (later she became a nurse); Mart had a respectable job as night agent for Railway Express. Of the older children, only Charlie seemed unable to settle down and accept what Galesburg could offer in the way of career and achievement. He made an effort to accept his hometown by working briefly as a reporter for the Galesburg *Daily Mail*, but somehow the town's horizons seemed too limited to him.

Sandburg's incomplete autobiography does not reach this time of his life and does not therefore supply an explanation for the rejected diploma. But we can speculate that perhaps it was the result of the same instinct that, earlier in his college years, had caused him to reject fraternity membership and to organize instead a club for non-fraternity students. This was his protest against what he felt was the undemocratic nature of fraternal exclusivity.

His rejection of the sheepskin may also have been another phase of his one-young-man protest movement against the complacent American bourgeois society of that Victorian era. For several years his sympathies had lain totally outside the accepted standards of society, and he had for some time believed in the movements of Socialism and Populism. His heroes were the self-educated Lincoln, the "Great Commoner" Bryan, the freethinking Ingersoll, and, more recently, the often unschooled, daring organizers of the radical forces that were beginning to make an impact on the nation.

Was it not natural, then, for such an idealistic, yet paradoxically practical, young man to accept the customary and desirable higher education and then to reject its symbol—the piece of paper that serves so many young people as the passport into middle-class society? Being the kind of gut, rather than brain, thinker he was always to be, this was the romantic decision we might have expected of him. It was his way of informing the world that it was not the way he felt it should be.

Perhaps, too, he feared the temptations inherent in that impressive sheet of parchment. With that bachelor's degree in his pocket, might not the time come when lean days as a radical reformer or a vagabond poet would weaken his resolve and tempt him to use his diploma as the document of surrender to values he rejected? Under its spell he might even decide to become an advertising man (had he not once succumbed to the faith healer's easy money?), a young business

TOP LEFT *Sandburg lived intermittingly with his family in their fourth home—Turn of the Century house—until he left Galesburg permanently in 1905.*

TOP RIGHT *Sandburg, age twenty-four, in the spring of 1902 after leaving college.*

BELOW *Sandburg hopped this streetcar to get to his classes.*

OPPOSITE *Sandburg was editor of Lombard's yearbook in 1901.*

THE CANNIBAL
—ITS EXECUTIONERS.

CHARLES AUGUST SANDBURG.
Editing Manager

FREDERICK DICKINSON.
Managing Editor

HUBERT ELBRIDGE PERRINE.
Artist.

We have written the tale of Lombard
For enlightened people's mirth
In jesting guise, but ye are wise,
And ye know what the jest is worth,

executive (he was undeniably a go-getter, in the vernacular of the day), or even a teacher (and how often did Professor Wright curse the day he abandoned the lusty real world for musty academe and warn his youthful disciple against such a course?).

So he took to the road again, with something like Candide's best of all possible worlds—his cake both eaten and possessed. He had his education, yet he had not compromised his standing as a young radical proletarian poet. Surely, there was an insatiable romantic in him, as his writing soon proved and as his lifelong projection of his image of himself as poet affirmed. (One of his acquaintances recalled years later how, as a famous old poet waiting in the wings to go on for a reading, he carefully mussed his hair and brought that wayward lock down over his forehead before taking to the stage.)

He hopped a freight that summer of 1902 and this time journeyed east. He paused in New Jersey long enough to earn money for food by selling stereoscopic views to farmers. Then he moved on to New York City, where, on the basis of his college and Galesburg newspaper experience, he got a job for six weeks as a police reporter with the New York *Daily News* (not the predecessor of the present newspaper). His spare time was devoted to feverishly writing prose and poetry, page after page. Some of his writings reflected the influence of Elbert Hubbard, to whose home in East Aurora, New York, Sandburg made a pilgrimage with a letter of introduction from Professor Wright.

Off and on, he returned to Chicago to work for such diverse journals as *Unity* (a magazine of the Unitarian Church) and a short-lived magazine called *Tomorrow*. And all the time he was listening to the people talk and jotting down the lyrics of their songs and learning to play them on the guitar.

He spent nearly two years wandering—a period whose itinerary is obscure. This vagrant existence came to end in 1904, at McKees Rocks, Pennsylvania, where he and eight other hoboes were arrested for riding a freight train illegally. They were herded from a gondola by sheriff's officers and hustled off to Allegheny County Courthouse, where Sandburg was shackled to a Negro hobo for trial before a justice of the peace. The judge ignored Sandburg's plea for leniency because he was a Spanish-American War veteran and sentenced him to ten days in jail along with the other prisoners.

This incident lessened his enthusiasm for the road, and after he was freed, he returned to Galesburg and his old job in the fire department. Sandburg resumed his friendship with Professor Wright. He was twenty-six now, and if his family failed to understand his longings, he had no doubts about what he wanted to do. He showed the writings he had completed on the road to Professor Wright, who was impressed by them and published them for Sandburg under the colophon of Wright's Asgard Press, hand-set by Wright in Old Caslon type on Wright's basement press.

The first was a thirty-nine-page booklet, *In Reckless Ecstasy,* printed in 1904. Sandburg took the title from a quotation by Marie Corelli: "Ideas which cannot be stated in direct words may be brought home in reckless ecstasies of thought."

In a foreword, Professor Wright wrote of his student that he "reads everything, Boccaccio, Walt Whitman, Emerson, Tolstoi . . . . But literature, even at its best, is but a palled reflection of life; he prefers impressions at first hand."

In this early effort Sandburg wrote such things as: "I glory in this world of men and women, torn with troubles and lost in sorrow, yet living on to love and laugh and play through it all. My eyes range with pleasure over flowers, prairies, woods, grass, and running water, and the sea, and the sky and the clouds."

In an essay, called "Good Fooling," in this booklet, Sandburg's earliest published writing about Lincoln appeared: "Jollying is a fine art. The capacity for good fooling is an attribute of every beloved Master among men, and in proof history presents no more sublime and touching instance than Abraham Lincoln. My prayer is that I may be a good fool."

An occasional phrase in these early works hinted of Sandburg's promise. In a piece called "Millville," about a town in southern New Jersey where there was a glass factory, he wrote: "By day and by night, the fires burn on in Millville and bid the sand let in the light." But, budding social critic that he was, he also took note that the unionized glass-blowers earned $15 to $20 a week, whereas the unorganized carrying boys were paid only $2.50 to $3 a week.

In 1905, Wright printed two more booklets of Sandburg's writings as paperbacks with buckram covers. *The Plaint of a Rose* was bedecked with flowers hand-painted by Wright. It was a sentimental account of a dying flower's vain effort to compete for survival with the healthy rose which overshadowed it. The other booklet, *Incidentals,* was a collection of short pieces of an inspirational nature à la Elbert Hubbard.

Carl Sandburg

In one of them, "Apologia," Sandburg admitted that one day he might recall these little essays as "youthful impertinences," and he commented, "Life is more vast and strange than anything written about it—words are only incidentals." Echoes of his knockabout years sounded in such sentences as: "The hopes of youth have been scorched and scarred in me, but the romance of life has not burnt out nor the glory of living been extinguished. I may keep this boy heart of mine, with tears for the tragic, love for the beautiful, laughter at folly, and silent, reverent contemplation of the common and everyday mysteries."

He spoke against violence and on behalf of learning and knowledge. He hailed the common man as the true source of democracy's strength, for the "great man . . . who gives the world some great thought, some great action, something of use, beauty, or inspiration, comes up from the mob. . . ." Of poetry, he wrote: "We feel and see a thing before we study and explain it. Vision precedes analysis. That is why poets are as important as scientists." Of idealism: "I am an idealist. I can see humanity blundering on toward some splendid goal. . . . I am an idealist. I don't know where I'm going but I'm on my

LEFT *Sandburg (right) takes an order for stereoscopic views from class-mate Fred Dickinson.*

RIGHT *Fifty copies of Sandburg's first published work,* In Reckless Ecstasy, *were printed and bound in Professor Wright's basement in 1904.*

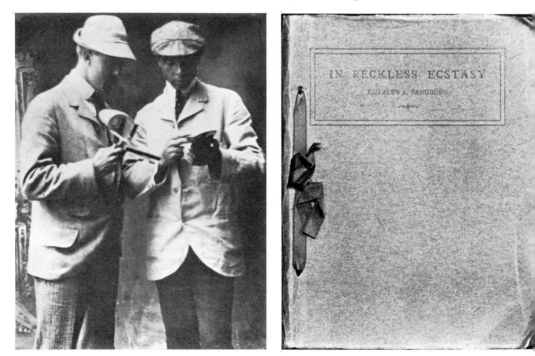

The
PLAINT
of a ROSE

SANDBURG

LEFT *Professor Wright set the type for* The Plaint of a Rose *(1905) and for the other Asgard Press paperbacks.*

ABOVE *Charlie Krans, Carl's best friend during the early years.*

way." He offered slogans: "Neither history nor newspapers surprise me any more," and "To get up and go on when you're knocked down is to get someplace."

In 1906, Wright published a booklet of his own writings, *The Dial of the Heart*, to which Sandburg responded with a foreword, in which he wrote, "Dream with the dreamer herein his dreams. Some day we may weave them into realities, for much of life is of such stuff as dreamers are made of." In his prologue to his poem "The Dreamer," Wright wrote, perhaps with Sandburg in mind:

> He shall come, the great Singer, and men shall be filled with
>   a new hope;
> He shall come, the great Singer, and the souls of men shall be
>   caught up as in a strong wind.

By this time Sandburg had become only an occasional visitor to Galesburg. He had stretched his horizons to Chicago. But he never forgot Wright, who in 1910 published one last work of Sandburg under the Asgard imprint, *Joseffy*, an appreciation of the poetry of a friend. In it, Sandburg preached the necessities of illusion to lighten life's hard realities.

Thirty years later, after Professor Wright's death in 1934, Sandburg composed a eulogy for his mentor that was included in a memorial booklet published by Wright's family:

> Philip Green Wright will always be a momentous figure to me. . . . He was a man of great and versatile intellect, so versatile that he was indifferent to the species of greatness that requires acclaim. I had four years of almost daily contact with him at college, for many years visited him as often as possible, and there never was a time when he did not deepen whatever reverence I had for the human mind. . . . He was a great man and teacher in his profound influence on the potential young men with whom he came in contact. Many of these will always bless his memory and keep it green.

5

The Young Radical

AMERICA in the first decade of the twentieth century was still living, as far as most of her citizens were concerned, in an age of innocence. Most of the country had not matured past the nineteenth century, when the United States had been able to nestle in the security of its Monroe Doctrine and when the merchants, bankers, industrialists, and other magnates in their heaven proclaimed all was right with the world. But for those who were alert to the social ferment that was working, it was an exciting era of revolutionary change.

These were the years when the great muckrakers were at work. Ida M. Tarbell was laying bare the sins of rampant capitalism in such works as *History of the Standard Oil Company*, and Lincoln Steffens was describing the miserable life of the poor in *The Shame of the Cities*. Supported by a $500 grant from the Socialist weekly *Appeal to Reason*, Upton Sinclair lived in the Chicago stockyards district and witnessed the brute existence of the slaughterhouse workers. The result was his sensational novel *The Jungle*, which shocked Americans who were willing to have their eyes pried open. Frank Norris was telling the truth about big business. Jack London was shouting angrily about the wrongs done to labor, and journalists—among them Charles Edward Russell, Ray Stannard Baker, and Tom Lawson—were turning society inside out in order to flaunt its soiled linen.

This was the time of the great union organizing drives, led by such controversial figures as the Socialist Eugene Debs, labor organizer "Mother" Jones, and Big Bill Haywood of the Industrial Workers of the World ("Wobblies"), whose slogan was "One Big Union."

This was the world that Sandburg was discovering and the kind of activity toward which his Socialist sympathies would direct him. Sandburg went to work as a reporter for the Chicago *Daily Socialist*. Its dimly lighted offices were located on Randolph Street in downtown Chicago, not far from State Street, where horse-drawn carriages and streetcars vied with early automobiles to cause some memorable traffic jams.

Reuben W. Borough, who later became an important figure in the Progressive Party, was another young radical drawn to the *Daily Socialist's* staff. In his unpublished autobiography, an excerpt from which appeared recently in the Chicago *Daily News*, he recalled his fellow staffer, Charles A. Sandburg, in 1905, as a "tall, gaunt young man smiling quizzically" with whom he was much impressed because some of Sandburg's poems had appeared in *Tomorrow* Magazine.

Sandburg was not a "scientific socialist" then, Borough wrote, "but

LEFT *In 1907 Carl Sandburg became a member of the Social Democratic Party of Wisconsin. His membership card indicates that he was spelling his name Sandberg at the time.*

RIGHT You and Your Job *(1908) is a social indictment against classic capitalism, and it is the most intense and agitated prose Sandburg has ever written.*

LEFT *Eugene Victor Debs (1855–1926), Socialist delegate to the third party conference, in his room at Lindlahr Sanitarium in Elmhurst, Illinois, 1924.*

RIGHT *Clarence Seward Darrow (1857–1938). Sandburg's great friendship with the famous lawyer was formed when they fought together on the side of the underdog during a workers' strike.*

he made up for the lack with sudden flashes of humor and outbursts of indignation and anger over the wrongs to the workingclass. . . . He was as militant and equalitarian as I was, and we were stubbornly committed to a proud identification with the poor and disinherited, and at war with capitalism."

Sandburg then was "in a period of brooding and gestation, evolving his rhyme-free poetry in solitude. Occasionally he would lay a specimen before me, neatly calligraphic though inscribed in lead pencil on cheap tablet paper, and ask for my opinion. I was convinced from the strength and beauty of his lines that he was a great creative artist."

Sandburg and Borough visited Hull House, where they spoke with the great Jane Addams, founder of the settlement house. Borough never forgot the vision of Sandburg's roughhewn profile raised in silent awe to study a heroic mural of Count Lee Tolstoy, in peasant boots and blouse, plowing a field. With another Socialist comrade, a harness maker named Mance, Sandburg and Borough made a trip to the saloon of the powerful First Ward alderman, Michael "Hinky Dink"

Kenna—one of the City Council's notorious "Gray Wolves," who controlled graft and patronage in Chicago. Sandburg was enthralled by the sight of the tough crowd quaffing big goblets of beer and downing the free lunch, but Borough was distressed by the stench rising from the damp sawdust on the floor.

Sandburg's wanderlust got the better of him again, and one day he packed his stereoscopic views and left for a selling swing through Illinois and Indiana. He picked up a little additional income by lecturing on Walt Whitman in any town that gave him the opportunity. At stops along his route, he wrote to Borough. From Hinckley, Illinois, he wrote: "Hinckley, isn't it musical? . . . Like Barbizon and Heidelberg. Green-crested hills surround the town and white roads lead off into gray mysterious distances. I shall be in dire peril of tossing off a poem or two." Again from Hinckley, his letter read: "It is quiet here. I think heaven is like Hinckley, with you and me and Mance each with a woman he loves as citizens." His landlady there, he confided, was afraid that "the socialists is likely to break out agin—ain't that awful?"

In his final letter to Borough, on July 9, 1907, Sandburg wrote: "Tell Mance when he dies I will lay a sword on his coffin and say he was a good soldier in the war for the liberation of mankind." Then he said that he would do the same for Borough and added, "I hope you can do as much for me—we are The Three Musketeers."

Sandburg's lecturing led him to an editorial post on *The Lyceumite* (a periodical for platform artists), and he was soon made its associate editor. For the publication, he wrote biographical sketches of the lecturers who were traveling various circuits, and whenever he was given the opportunity, he himself accepted a speaking engagement. His subjects were "The Poet of Democracy: Walt Whitman"; "Civilization and the Mob," a reflection of his Populist sentiments; and "Bernard Shaw: Artist and Fool."

In the winter of 1907 he met Winfield R. Gaylord, an organizer for the Social Democratic Party in Wisconsin, whose talk of fieldwork fired Sandburg with enthusiasm. Gaylord offered Sandburg a chance to work as a party organizer, and Sandburg accepted. He moved to Milwaukee, where he was trained in political organizing techniques. He traveled the lake region of Wisconsin, earning about $25 a month by passing the hat after his talks to the factory hands and farmers who attended party rallies. He also wrote a few Social Democratic pamphlets that sold for 5 cents each, and he earned another few dollars a month this way. Occasionally, he was able to sell an article to *La Follette's Weekly* for $100.

Theodore Roosevelt was in the White House, battling the monopolists who exploited the people. Wisconsin was in the vanguard of the Progressive movement, with its Senator, the elder Robert La Follette (former three-time governor of Wisconsin) supporting Roosevelt's reform efforts and with ardent Socialists, such as Emil Seidel and Victor Berger, becoming influential figures in the state.

Sandburg moved from town to town, carrying little but the pamphlets and party membership applications his work required and a change of clothes. He would leave his dirty linens at the first stop on a circuit to be laundered by the wife of a friendly Socialist and pick them up on the way back. The only unnecessary weight he lugged with him was his volumes of Shakespeare, Whitman, and Emerson.

He was preaching radical solutions for the nation's social ills— doctrines which were not to become acceptable for another three decades. The Socialist program called for controversial reforms such as an eight-hour workday, old-age pensions, unemployment insurance, industrial accident insurance, a guaranteed annual minimum wage, higher wages, abolition of child labor, laws to protect and encourage unionism, and free textbooks for public schools.

One day in Milwaukee in 1907, when Sandburg was visiting the office of Victor Berger, the state's Social Democratic Party leader and a member of Congress, he met a lovely dark-haired young woman with soft gray eyes, for whom he formed an immediate affection. Lillian Steichen was the daughter of immigrants from Luxembourg and a Phi Beta Kappa graduate of the University of Chicago. A teacher at the Princeton (Illinois) Township High School, she had returned to Wisconsin to spend the Christmas vacation with her parents in Menomonee Falls and had come to Milwaukee to offer to translate into English some of Berger's editorials written for a German-language publication. When she left the office, Sandburg invited himself to accompany her to the streetcar.

After that, they saw each other as frequently as their duties permitted. Whenever Miss Steichen returned to Wisconsin to visit her family, Sandburg managed to visit her. They both were eager young Socialists, and they also shared a love of literature. By now poetry was Sandburg's major interest, and he showed his free verse experiments to Miss Steichen, who was attempting to create what she called "word-

75

melodies." What Wright had been for Sandburg, Thorstein Veblen (the University of Chicago economist who created shibboleths for the rebels of his generation, such as "conspicuous consumption," "vicarious leisure," and "conspicuous waste") had been for the brilliant young woman.

Lillian's middle-class parents were slightly shocked by the vagabond Socialist with whom their daughter had fallen in love, but Sandburg found an ally in Lillian's brother, Edward Steichen, who was engaged in tedious experiments with lighting and angles, chemicals, and printing papers. Edward's successful experimentation enabled him to become one of the great photographers of his time.

The Steichens called their daughter Paus'l, a Luxembourg term of endearment that meant kitten, and Sandburg with his penchant for nicknames soon changed that to Paula. Because she preferred the shorter and more virile Carl to either Charles or Charlie, Sandburg bowed to her preference.

On June 15, 1908, after the school year ended, Paula and Carl Sandburg were married. They moved to Appleton, Wisconsin, into a three-room upstairs apartment, whose rent was $4 a month, and Paula managed to furnish it with a cheap bed and mattress, two chairs, a table, and a few packing crates for storage. Whenever it was possible, she traveled with Carl on his organizing rounds. A story in the Chicago *Daily Socialist*—on July 7, 1908, from "Menominee Springs," told how some local farmhands decided to toss a charivari for the newlyweds outside a farmhouse where the couple was sleeping. It also told how the young organizer outwitted them.

Clanging cowbells and tin cans and blowing horns, the rowdies shouted their demands for money to buy beer and cigars as tribute from the bridgegroom. Instead, Sandburg came out to treat them with a Socialist speech about the plight of the poor workman, and he ended it:

> "If I had a million dollars . . ." Cries of "We wish you had!"
> "I would not give you one cent for beer and cigars. A Social Democrat gives his money to the cause he is fighting for. The Social Democratic Party of Wisconsin has no traction companies to support it. A little from each man will help. We depend on the workingman for support."
> Then he passed the hat. Some paid and others walked away. They gave one last grand chorus of noise—a sort of infernal finale—and then a cheer for Social Democracy.

ABOVE *4646 North Hermitage, where Carl and Paula Sandburg took their first Chicago apartment on the second floor.*

BELOW *Harriet Monroe at her desk at* Poetry *Magazine.*

Carl Sandburg

The Sandburgs carried their liberal notions over into their marriage. Not only was no ring used in the ceremony to bind them; but the word "obey" was eliminated from the ritual, and substituted for it was an agreement that their contract would cease to be binding if either of them ever wanted to void the union. Some years later, after a quarrel, Paula reminded Carl of this prerogative and invited him to make use of it if he wished. "I'll be damned if I'll go through all that courting again," he replied.

That year Sandburg wrote a pamphlet, *You and Your Job*, which was published by the Socialist Party and sold for 5 cents. His byline was still "Charles Sandburg," as it was to remain for some years, although his wife and friends had taken to calling him Carl. The pamphlet opened with a folksy "Dear Bill: Your last letter is here, the one in which you talk about the man who is out of a job. You say, Bill, that the man . . . has only himself to blame," and it went on to explain the Socialist theory about how such a workman was the victim of the capitalist system. "I believe in obstacles, but I say that a system such as the capitalist system, putting such obstacles as starvation, underfeeding, overwork, bad housing and perpetual uncertainty of work in the lives of human beings, is a pitiless, ignorant, blind, reckless, cruel mockery of a system."

In the pamphlet he went on to urge the Socialist remedies for social ills. These were legitimized in the Democratic Party platforms of 1932 and afterward, and Sandburg concluded, "If the capitalists will not provide, the government must." Again, he was some years ahead of his times.

A married man with responsibilties, Sandburg had to think about improving his family's living standard. The Sandburgs moved in 1909 to Milwaukee, where Carl wrote advertising copy for a department store. He also composed half a dozen newspaper feature stories, which he submitted to the Milwaukee *Journal*. Impressed by the stories, the newspaper hired him. He was a reporter for the *Journal* for only a brief time before he was hired by the Milwaukee *Daily News* as an editorial writer to fill in for a regular man who was vacationing. For the *News*, he wrote an editorial praising the government's good judgment in putting Lincoln's profile on the common man's coin—the penny.

After a short stretch on the Milwaukee *Sentinel*, Sandburg returned to the *Journal* as its City Hall reporter. There he became acquainted with Emil Seidel, the Socialist leader who was running for mayor of Milwaukee. Sandburg campaigned on Seidel's behalf, speaking on street corners and at Socialist rallies, and when Seidel was swept into office, his first appointment was Sandburg as his private secretary. (In Schenectady, New York, in the same year, another young liberal, Walter Lippmann, was named secretary to Socialist mayor-elect George R. Lunn.)

One of Sandburg's colleagues in the new Socialist regime described him, because of his sincere approach to the people's problems, with the phrase "He's got the heart of a mother." One of his first chores in his new post was to listen to the complaint of a voter about a dead dog in the alley by his house. Sandburg called the proper city department and had the carcass removed. Perhaps Sandburg's most trying burden as the mayor's secretary—one that he remembered with distaste for long years to come—was to serve as a buffer between Mayor Seidel and seekers of patronage jobs. With all his other obligations, Sandburg endured in his attempts to develop an individual style of poetry and prose. Sometimes he showed one of his efforts to the mayor, who patted him on the back and said, "That's fine, Carl."

Early in 1910, Carl's father, August Sandburg, fell from a ladder while trimming a tree in the backyard of his home in Galesburg. He never recovered from the injury, developed pneumonia, and died on March 22, 1910. His eldest son wrote of August Sandburg in *Always the Young Strangers:* "No glory of any kind ever came to him. I am quite sure his name was never printed till he died and there was a brief obituary—and in the paragraph about his funeral his name was spelled 'Andrew' instead of 'August.' Yet there is an affirmative view that can be taken of his life, not merely affirmative but somewhat triumphant." August Sandburg had found life satisfying. He had enjoyed good health until the accident, and he was never dishonest. "Peace be to your ashes, Old Man. . ." Sandburg wrote, then adding about both his parents, "Yes, peace to your dust and clods of earth. You were givers of life and did no wrong by any you met on your mortal pilgrimage."

In 1911, Paula gave birth to Margaret, the first of the Sandburgs' three daughters, increasing Sandburg's need for a larger income. He left his political job with Seidel in 1912 to become labor reporter for the Milwaukee *Leader,* the state's leading Socialist newspaper, and he was a crusading journalist.

His stories were notable for outspokenness. A typical story—

ABOVE *A page from the April, 1916, issue of the* Review *in which Sand-burg had four poems: "Gone," "Graves," "Choice," and "Child of the Romans."*

OPPOSITE *He had a massive frame and a face cut out of stone.*

headlined "Joe Carney, Why Don't You Tell People about $600,000 Graft in Asphalt Pavement?"—showed that Sandburg was a capable muckraker. His article explained in detail how Carney, chairman of the committee of streets and alleys under the previous administration, had paid one and one-half times as much for asphalt as Mayor Seidel's people had paid, and Sandburg concluded:

> . . . somebody got graft of at least sixty cents a yard on all asphalt pavements in Milwaukee for the past ten years.
>
> Joe Carney may stand in Oscar Liebner's saloon and gulp whiskey and tell his friends that the Socialists are "free lovers." And he may stand before an audience and tell them "Old Glory" is a grand old flag. But on the subject of paving as a matter of public business we have the right to say that all the records show this and show it clear as daylight.
>
> Joe Carney is either a tool and a grafter; or else, he is an ignorant lunkhead in public service. There are no other alternatives.

Later that year a newspaper pressmen's strike in Chicago shut down the major dailies, and the Chicago *Daily Socialist* became the only newspaper publishing. It changed its name, to take advantage of this opportunity, to the Chicago *World*, and, as the only paper in town, its modest circulation climbed to 600,000 a day during the strike. With all its new business, it needed additional staff members, and Sandburg moved his family from Milwaukee to go to work for the *World*. He had always wanted to become a reporter for a major Chicago newspaper, for, as Paula said some years later, "Chicago and Carl were made for each other."

They found a second-floor apartment in an old rambling gray frame house on the Northwest Side, but almost as soon as they were settled, the pressmen's strike was over. The other dailies resumed publication, the *World's* circulation tumbled, and Sandburg was out of a job. Desperate, Sandburg spent a few weeks vainly seeking work so he could support his family and he recalled later of this time, "I'd often been broke before, but this was different, I now knew something of the terror of an unemployed man with a family. It was amazing to think of how few people there were in that great city to whom I could turn even for a very small loan."

Finally, he was hired at $25 a week by E. W. Scripps' experimental—and liberal—adless newspaper *The Day Book*. With its work-

ingmen's sympathies, *The Day Book* provided Sandburg with the ideal
outlet for the expression of his social and political beliefs. He was free
to write the truth as he saw it—a rare opportunity in journalism that he
was again to enjoy, a few years later, when he joined the Chicago
Daily News.

In his spare time he continued to create poetry. Paula, out of her
great faith in his genius, kept mailing his poems to a variety of magazines, but with little success.

Perhaps Sandburg's brief brush with unemployment was responsible for his next move. In 1913 he made a rare compromise with
his principles and went to work for a capitalist publication—*System*
Magazine—designed to guide business and industry in a more efficient
use of workers and equipment. Although Sandburg was earning $10
a week more than *The Day Book* had been paying him, his heart was
not in it, and he worked at *System* for only a few months.

(Years later, however, he was to acknowledge a debt to the business techniques he learned at *System.* When he was engulfed for years
in his great Lincoln biography, he found that the organizational and
filing techniques of which he had written at *System* were helpful to
him in creating an effective method for handling the voluminous data
he accumulated about Lincoln and his times.)

From *System,* he bounced briefly to the *National Hardware
Journal* and then to *American Artisan* before he returned to *The Day
Book.* And all the time he was creating poetry. He said later of this
period, "Wherever an idea for a poem hit me I put it down in pencil,
then worked over it at my leisure." For example, his famous little poem
"Fog" (its techniques inspired by Sandburg's admiration of the imag-
ist achievements of haiku poetry) was scribbled while he was waiting
in an anteroom of Juvenile Court to see the judge.

The Sandburg's second daughter, Janet, was born in 1914, and the
family moved to an old large house in suburban Maywood. Paula Sandburg made another notable contribution to the Sandburg fortunes that
year when she mailed a sheaf of nine of Carl's poems to Harriet Monroe's bold little publication *Poetry: A Magazine of Verse.* Miss Monroe's friend and aide Alice Corbin opened the parcel of poems and was
impressed with the originality and strength of Sandburg's unorthodox
free verse. She showed them to Miss Monroe, who wrote of this discovery in her autobiography, *A Poet's Life:*

Carl Sandburg

Alice had handed over to me a group of strange poems in very individual free verse, beginning with "Chicago" as "hog-butcher of the world." This line was a shock at first, but I took a long breath and swallowed it, and was laughed at scornfully by critics and columnists when we gave it the lead in March, 1914.

She went on to recall the Sandburg of that time, at thirty-six, as:

. . . a typical Swedish peasant of proletarian sympathies . . . with a massive frame and a face cut out of stone. . . . His delicate-featured very American wife told me that ours was the first acceptance of Carl's poems, although for two years she had been collecting rejection slips from a steady campaign against editors. Carl would come in often to sit solidly in our "poet's chair," and talk of life and poetry with whoever might be there, weighing his words before risking utterance in his rich, low-pitched, quiet voice.

For these verses Sandburg was paid $100, the greatest amount he had earned from his poetry. It also marked his entry into what was then probably the most exciting literary milieu in the United States. It was the Chicago that a few years later H. L. Mencken christened "the literary capital of the world." The Chicago school earned the name by spawning Theodore Dreiser, Ring Lardner, Sherwood Anderson, Edgar Lee Masters, Vachel Lindsay, Ben Hecht, Lloyd Lewis, Charles MacArthur, Sandburg, and several others, as well as champions of controversial new talents, such as Harriet Monroe and Margaret Anderson, founder of *The Little Review*, in which so many of the new writers achieved their publishing debuts.

At the end of 1914 Miss Monroe was instrumental in the selection of Sandburg as the winner of the Helen Haire Levinson Prize of $200 for the best poetry published that year. In retrospect, there is irony in the controversy that Sandburg's virile free verse caused. Only a few months later, in June, 1915, *Poetry* gave T. S. Eliot his first American publication with "The Love Song of J. Alfred Prufrock," and this created little excitement although it had introduced to the cultural scene the subjective, intellectual brilliance of truly modern poetry, which was to leave all verse behind in the coming decade.

That year, 1914, was one of the most crucial to Sandburg's future. He had been officially launched when his poems appeared in *Poetry* Magazine. Finally, at thirty-six, his vagabond years of search and trial were behind him. He had reached the threshold of his long creative years.

84

6

Newspaperman

ONE day in the summer of 1914 a friend took Carl Sandburg to the press room of the County Building in Chicago to introduce him to some of the reporters for the big daily newspapers. Boasting that Sandburg was a genius, the friend urged Carl to read some of his poetry to the press room gang. His unorthodox verse was not hailed with much enthusiasm, but a young reporter for the Chicago *Daily News* appreciated it. That was Ben Hecht, a legendary name in the boisterous Chicago newspaper world of the era. Hecht was impressed not only by Sandburg's virile poetry but also by the poet's passionate delivery. From that day forward Hecht became one of Sandburg's staunchest friends and champions, even if he never fully understood the poet's manner.

Another early Sandburg supporter was the budding genius Ezra Pound, who was living in England and had read Sandburg's poems in *Poetry* Magazine. In January, 1915, in one of his long letters to Harriet Monroe, in which he sought to help her discover and nurture deserving talent, Pound hailed her youthful discovery (Sandburg was thirty-seven then) as a poet of considerable promise—if, Pound added, Sandburg could only learn to write.

Poetry's Alice Corbin felt no such qualifications were necessary to describe Sandburg's gifts. In the fall of 1915 she traveled to New York City to leave a packet of Sandburg's poems with Alfred Harcourt, a

TOP *Newspaperman.*

BELOW LEFT *Carl Sandburg, age thirty-nine, 1917.*

BELOW RIGHT *Chicago* Daily News *building, on Wells, near Madison Street, 1917.*

salesman for the book publishing firm of Henry Holt and Company. Harcourt later wrote of his reaction to Sandburg's poetry:

> I saw at once that it was of the first importance and quality. There was something of a skirmish to get it past the inhibitions and traditions of the Holt office for its middle-western atmosphere, its subject matter and strength seemed to them rather raw for their imprint, but Henry Holt himself agreed to let me try it. . . .

Chicago Poems was published in the spring of 1916, thanks to Harcourt's vigorous effort. Miss Monroe praised the strength and honesty of these poems, some of which appeared first in *Poetry*. It was verse of "massive gait," she said, "whether you call it poetry or not." She called it poetry. So did Amy Lowell, who wrote in *The New York Times:* " 'Chicago Poems' is one of the most original books this age has produced." In *Poetry Review*, the reviewer concluded that "Carl Sandburg has shaped poetry that is like a statue by Rodin."

The enthusiasm, however, was far from unanimous. The influential critical review *The Dial* (in which Sandburg's poems had been brutally scored two years earlier upon their publication in *Poetry*) reaffirmed its earlier aversion. Sandburg was "gross, simple-minded, sentimental, sensual," a confused "mystical mobocrat" simultaneously defending and attacking contemporary culture. Stanley Braithwaite in the Boston *Transcript* acknowledged Sandburg's "tenderness" and "visual strength," but he concluded that the poems were "ill-regulated speech that has neither verse nor prose rhythms."

Despite, or perhaps as a result of, this lack of critical consensus, Sandburg had suddenly become one of the most controversial poets in the nation. When his work was criticized for its unvarnished bluntness, he liked to say, "Here is the difference between Dante, Milton and me. They wrote about hell and never saw the place. I wrote about Chicago after looking the town over for years and years."

With his first volume of published verse, Sandburg earned entry into the Chicago coterie of writers and poets. But he was never to become an esthete who scorned the concerns of everyday people, for he belonged to another, more vital milieu—that of the working newspaperman. And although some of his colleagues recalled his idealism and his poetry with good-natured contempt, the old, yellowed clippings of his news and feature stories prove that he was a gifted journalist.

There are wonderful anecdotes about Sandburg the poet-reporter.

ABOVE   *In 1918, when Carl Sandburg fell heir to Eugene Field's old desk, the* News *was still using a few horse-drawn delivery wagons.*

BELOW   *Columnist Lloyd Lewis (left) with Henry Justin Smith, managing editor of the Chicago* Daily News, *1918.*

One, preserved by Albert Parry, is of the time Sandburg, for *The Day Book*, and Hecht, for the *Daily News*, journeyed to Wheaton, Illinois, to cover the execution of a murderer. During the journey to the western suburb, they argued the merits of vers libre versus traditional poetry, and the debate continued as they waited at the press telegraph table near the gallows. When the doomed man, Harry Spencer, had mounted to the scaffold and was asked if he had any last words to utter, he began to recite, "The Lord is my Shepherd, I shall not want. . . ." Then, according to Parry, Sandburg pinched Hecht under the table and whispered, "Listen! What better authority do you want? Pure vers libre and in the Bible!"

On July 6, 1917, *The Day Book* ceased publication. America had entered World War I, and Scripps had decided that his adless newspaper was too expensive an experiment to carry on, especially in a time when its social criticism might hinder, rather than help, the war effort. In its last issue, Sandburg wrote an analysis of the causes of the bloody East St. Louis, Illinois, race riot. They were the fault not so much of the white rioters of that city as of Armour and the other packinghouse companies, which "make a specialty of importing southern Negroes to work alongside white men in the north." Also at fault, he wrote, was "an East St. Louis aluminum factory, which has had hundreds of white men on strike for months and is using Negroes freshly imported from the south to fill the places of the strikers."

The National Labor Defense League, an organization financed by liberals who wanted to be sure that labor's side would be given in disputes, hired Sandburg to work as a troubleshooter. He traveled for the league to Omaha and to St. Louis to serve as a spokesman for striking workers.

Then, for one of the few times in his life, he succumbed to the temptation of money against the prompting of his sympathies. He was offered a salary of $100 a week to work for William Randolph Hearst's Chicago *Evening American*. It was twice as much money as he had ever earned in a week, and Sandburg became a Hearstling, but only for a few weeks. "I didn't belong," he said years later. "They had their own way of doing things. My way didn't fit theirs. After three weeks I quit and went to the Chicago *Daily News*, cutting my pay in two."

Ben Hecht was to claim credit for uniting Sandburg and the *News*. He said that after he learned that Sandburg was unemployed, he told Henry Justin Smith, the *News'* managing editor, "There's a good reporter you ought to hire." When Smith argued that the *News* was overstaffed, Hecht pressed on, "His name's Sandburg . . . and he's not only a good reporter but he writes superb poetry."

This was the way to Smith's heart. Remembered for years by alumni of his remarkable staff of the twenties as "the hard-boiled saint," his love of the *News* was equaled only by his worship of literature and of the gifted men who could create it. "What kind of poetry?" he asked Hecht.

"The new kind. . . . Like Walt Whitman. Wonderful stuff. . . ."

"Tell him to come around," Smith said curtly.

And Sandburg was hired. With the exception of a five-month assignment for the Newspaper Enterprise Association (N.E.A.) in 1918 and 1919, when he was sent to Sweden to report on the declining days of the war and the turmoil of the Russian Revolution, Sandburg remained with the *News* working for Smith for thirteen years.

Undoubtedly it was Smith's influence that kept Sandburg and the other phenomenal staff members with the *News*. Years later Harry Hansen wrote of that wonderful editor:

> It is my belief that neither Carl nor I would have lasted long on the newspaper but for the unusual protection assured us by Smith's interest. No one has yet done justice in print to this extraordinary genius of the newspaper. Only Smith could have held the loyalty of so many men and women and achieved distinction in literature and journalism. I can't begin to enumerate them.

Among them were Sandburg, Hecht, Hansen, John Gunther, Meyer Levin, Robert J. Casey, Vincent Starrett, and many others. Someone once tallied the achievements of Smith's staff: in eight years, twenty-five men and women published fifty books of poetry, fiction, criticism, drama, biography, and political and social science.

A number of the literati of Chicago's golden age were to write reminiscences of the Sandburg of his newspaper days. It was poet Witter Bynner who christened him "The Great Iron Cat" in a poem by that name:

OPPOSITE *Sandburg's obituary of Rudolph Valentino, 1926. Carl was motion picture editor for the Chicago* Daily News *at the time.*

FAR RIGHT TOP TO BOTTOM *Early newspaper photographs of "Sandy" Sandburg when he worked for Victor Lawson's Chicago* Daily News *under two great editors, Henry Justin Smith and, later, Charles Dennis.*

Girls' Idea of Prince Was Rudolph Valentino

BY CARL SANDBURG.

Rudolph Valentino's wide popularity, which this week is seen to have been a more amazing fame in extent than was at first supposed, traces back to a number of causes.

Rudy was the center of a romance of wealth, for one thing. In his earlier days on the screen he was referred to by rivals and envious commentators as "the dishwasher."

It may be that some people now as they pass a restaurant sign "Dishwasher Wanted" will pause to say: "Well, the one they get may rise —Valentino did."

Then, too, he embodied in a picturesque way something of sudden romance, of money not counted in tens of thousands nor hundreds of thousands, as the best of stage stars count it, but in millions. "Rudy? Oh, he made a million last year."

Then there was the gossip about him, there was his adventuring, changing, shifting, hunting for the woman he wanted, his first divorce that wasn't a divorce, so that he had to annul a marriage. And after that the woman whom he married, unmarried and remarried, finally had to be divorced. And while he was hinting that he had temperament and never would find the woman he wanted, a dark-haired Polish screen actress was announcing that he and she were betrothed.

Thus he was kept in the minds of people, many people. His actual screen audience may not have equaled that of Tommy Meighan; it certainly was not as large as that of Harold Lloyd. But Rudy called somehow to that vague, intangible thing called romance. A touch of the exquisite, carried sometimes to extravaganza, clung about him; no statistician can inform us how far he provoked or furthered the young male custom of slicking back the hair in what is called "the young sheik style."

He appealed to a wide audience of men and women, boys and girls, but chiefly women and girls, as having grace and personal charm. If they read stories saying, "The young prince was of comely features and a surpassing bodily grace," their first thought on trying to fix such a type in real life was of Rudolph Valentino.

> Aloof, but at home wherever men be,
> In town or on the prairie,
> Tender toeing round a child,
> Tigered with moonlight in the wild,
> Mysterious and more than that,
> Sandburg comes, the iron cat. . . .

And in one of his sensitive newspaper novels, *Deadlines,* published in 1923, Henry Justin Smith devoted one of his vignettes on newsroom characters to Sandburg. In the chapter "The Poet," Smith, as the anonymous Old Man, boasts that he has been able to keep Sandburg on his staff for five years:

A rightful boast. It is no joke to keep a poet anywhere.

> He has been happy, we think. As for us, we have seen poems born. We have watched The Poet at his window, lounging deep in his chair, his powerful hands knotted, his dark, rugged face locked in a solemn dream. The poems, themselves, have been on exhibition at various stages: as pencilled yellow slips, as clean sheets retyped for the printer, as long rolls of galley-proofs. . . . All this makes The Poet more incongruous than ever. Who is he, after all? A great man, or only one of us?

In *Deadlines* Smith creates a memorable portrait of Sandburg's enthusiasm for news and newspaper work. He shows Sandburg, heavy-footing it to the city desk to remark, "Some front page today—man, that's journalism!" He shows Sandburg sharing eagerly in the news of a "big scoop, a grievous quarrel, or a new baby. He is interested in the people of the news-room; and he has periods of absorption in news itself."

Then, at length, Smith re-creates an evening at Le Petit Gourmet —one of the local hangouts of the Chicago literati, along with Schlogl's Restaurant, the Dill Pickle Club, and the Covici-McGee Book Store. The crowd has gathered when Sandburg arrives late, "muffled to the eyes" with a heavy scarf and his "black rain-proof cap, which is so ugly that he idolizes it." Then the poet accedes to requests to read for his friends, poets and writers and journalists:

> It is a voice familiar enough, yet charged with a new element. It is a deep voice, deliberate, casual, rich with earth-tones. It comes as though some organist were idly exploring the pedals. . . .

Before their eyes, the familiar newsroom figure metamorphoses into another being—remote and inexplicable:

> Well, there is something we have overlooked. . . . The companionable chuckle with which he greets us is gone. He has a stern, white look that abashes us. Concentration is cutting that familiar face into hollows. . . . Comrades, we never fathomed him. There is something else here, and we can't quite describe it. And when The Poet has finished, we walk home in the peaceful night, convinced of the majesty of ourselves.

Hecht had a different image of Sandburg at this time—one more in keeping with the irreverent eyes Hecht leveled at every aspect of the world. He saw the poet humorously as a nemesis of hardheaded news editors, a dreamer in the hardheaded world of news gathering, trudging into the city room in his Galesburg cap with a faraway look in his eye that baffled practical city editor Brooks Beitler. George Wharton of the Associated Press identified the headgear as a "herring catcher's cap" and gave Sandburg the nickname John Guts. Hecht had read to Wharton a Sandburg poem in which a sweaty Italian railroad worker enjoys a sandwich beside the tracks as a streamliner flashes past with its elegant passengers eating royally in the dining car.

In those days, according to Hecht, Sandburg's passion for collecting evidence of the wisdom of the people kept his pockets jammed with scraps of paper, penciled notes, and yellowed newspaper clippings. Hecht told of one day when Sandburg walked to the city desk to thrust an eight-year-old clipping from a North Dakota newspaper at Beitler. The city editor stared at it in bewilderment and finally asked, "What about it?"

"The people of Fargo have got something," Sandburg said slowly and resonantly, as Hecht reported the incident.

Later Beitler said to Hecht, "I understand this fella's a genius. You got any idea what a genius can do?"

Another anecdote Hecht related was about the occasion when Sandburg was sent to Minneapolis to cover an American Federation of Labor convention. Three days passed with no word from Sandburg, and Smith kept trying to assuage Beitler's anxiety. On the fourth day, when a wire service story came through about a delegate's running amok, shooting a speaker, critically wounding him, and inspiring other delegates to draw guns and turn the session into a wild melee in which several people were wounded, Beitler asked Smith what he should do about Sandburg. Sighing, Smith said, "Tell him to come home."

Beitler dispatched a telegram to Sandburg with this order. An hour later Sandburg wired back: "Dear Boss. Can't leave now. Everything too important and exciting. Sandburg."

This was the image of Sandburg that Hecht wanted to preserve, and as affectionately as Hecht remembered his old colleague, it still seems to be an unfair evaluation. Sandburg's published stories for the *Daily News* create the image of a different kind of journalist—alert, talented, and responsible.

When Big Bill Haywood, leader of the Wobblies (for which Sandburg had delivered a few organizational speeches in his radical days in Wisconsin), was arrested in the Justice Department's controversial roundup of Wobblies and Socialists in World War I, Sandburg gained the first interview with Haywood and wrote:

> Through a steel cage door of the Cook County Jail, Big Bill Haywood today spoke the defiance of the Industrial Workers of the World to its enemies and captors.
>
> Bill didn't pound on the door, shake the iron clamps nor ask for pity nor make any kind of display as a hero. He peered through the square holes of the steel slats and talked in the even voice of a poker player who may or may not hold the winning hand. . . . The man accused of participation in ten thousand separate and distinct crimes lifted a face checkered by the steel lattice work and said with a slow smile: "Hello, I'm glad to see you. Do you know when they are going to bring the rest of the boys here? It would be homelike for all of us to be together. . . . Ten thousand crimes! If they can make the American people or any fair-minded jury believe that, I don't see how they'll do it. . . ." Haywood takes it easy. He discussed the ten thousand crimes with the massive leisure of Hippo Vaughn pitching a shut-out.

Although this news story shows that Sandburg maintained a warm attitude toward his old friend, he did not sympathize with the efforts of the Wobblies and Socialists to impede the war effort. A week after that article appeared, Sandburg and his wife resigned from the Socialist Party. It was after nearly twenty years of sympathy with its cause and a decade of active membership. The party refused to support America's entry into the war, and Sandburg, always the patriot, explained his resignation by saying, "I fight against wars between wars, but once we're in it, I give it everything I have." For the remainder of his life, he professed political independence, although he worked for the election of Democratic Presidential candidates Roosevelt, Truman, and Kennedy.

People who like to think of Sandburg as the earnest poet forget about his admiration of the "good fool" who leavened life's crises with wit, as Abraham Lincoln had done. Their assessment of Sandburg might be altered by an interview with Babe Ruth in the *Daily News* in March, 1919.

Sandburg asked the Babe for five rules of good conduct that the home run king's young fans might follow to prepare for a career in sports. The Babe prescribed plenty of sleep, the right foods, and no cigarettes or alcohol. "The Babe wouldn't think of two more and was willing to let it go at these three," Sandburg said. He then asked Ruth

LEFT *Sandburg, age forty-nine, when* The American Songbag *was released, 1927.*

RIGHT *Sandburg interviews actress Mary Carr Achen for his "Silver Screen" columns in the Roaring Twenties.*

what he would advise a boy who asked the baseball star which books to read:

> "I never get that. They don't ask me that question. They ask me how to play ball."
>
> If you were to name two or three books that you like a lot, what would they be?
>
> "I don't know. I like books with excitement, dramatic murders. . . ."
>
> Is there any one character in history you are especially interested in, such as Lincoln, Washington, Napoleon?
>
> "I've never seen any of them," he replied.

Sandburg was not to spend much more time, after May, 1919, as a reporter. Sensitive to the needs and potentials of his talented staff, Smith made Sandburg the paper's movie critic. By spending three crammed days viewing early silent movies, writing his reviews, and doing stories on Chaplin, Mary Pickford, and Valentino, Sandburg had the rest of the week to pursue his serious, personal work. This was his routine for nearly ten years until, after he himself had become a celebrity, he was given his own column, "Carl Sandburg's Notebook," in which to write about whatever interested him.

But before his stint as a working journalist was ended, he achieved one of the finest efforts of his career. With its consistently expert news sense, the *News* in the early summer of 1919 asked Sandburg to visit the city's crowded, growing Black Belt. In need of labor for war industry, the city was crammed with Negroes drawn from the South. Sandburg was asked to report on their lives and attitudes. His series on the Negro problem had been running in the *Daily News* for two weeks when a colored boy who had ventured to a whites-only South Side beach was stoned by whites and drowned. This incident instigated the terrible race riots in which twenty Negroes and fourteen whites were killed.

Much of what Sandburg wrote in that series is as timely today as it was nearly half a century ago. Negroes attempted to leave the overcrowded ghettos for better living areas, but frightened white people resisted integration. The volatile situation was aggravated by postwar unemployment, the return of disenchanted Negro veterans from the

OPPOSITE LEFT AND TOP RIGHT   *His "Notebook" columns appeared Wednesdays and Fridays.*

RIGHT BOTTOM   *He smoked his cigars so short that it looked as if his tobacco was on fire.*

N HIS younger days H. G. Wells wrote some books worth reading, ne of them a novel called "Tono ungay."

I mention it now because you may et be thinking on the question of hy Ivar Kreuger, the Swedish match ing, killed himself.

Of course, when any man kills im- elf it is often a secret with himself s to just why he chose to send him- elf across the border.

In the case of Ivar Kreuger, how- ver, it seems as though he followed course somewhat like that of the ain character in "Tono Bungay."

Each of them strayed into fields here a vast surplus income came lling in.

Each of them sought new fields for investment of the ever-fresh surplus earnings.

Each of them built a fabric that ecame a tower of Babel, a confusion tongues.

As the fabricated structure wabbled ward collapse the weaver of it lled himself.

It happens occasionally with big- y slickers and with small-town Na- leons.

I would advise the reading of H. G. ells' "Tono Bungay" by many young en and women.

And as I look back at Ivar Kreuger am sure he was not a type but an dividual, perhaps a very friendly man creature under the exterior serves of his financial face.

He had at least a touch of humor d whim, for when he was asked s advice as to how a young man ould go at it to win a fortune he plied, "Marry a rich widow."

* * *

WOMAN who manages the book department of a large store tells e they had been selling two or ree copies a day of "The Good arth." Then Will Rogers kicked er his rules and devoted all his ragraphs one day to a sweeping commendation of this book. "We ld ten copies that day," said our okseller lady. "We ran out of ock and telegraphed for more." As book reviewer who reviews one book ery five years, Will Rogers is all the good.

Carl Sandburg

FROM THE NOTEBOOK
of CARL SANDBURG

Chicago, Ill., May 30, 1930.

Carl Sandburg, care Chicago Daily News, Chicago, Ill.

The graduating class and students of Crane College Municipal College of Chicago request that your honor send a message of encouragement that may be published in our annual we will graduate several hundred students from Law arts commerce and engineering courses.

OTTO COELLN Editor Crane College Chicago.

ON RECEIVING the above telegram we laid it by for a day and then sat down and did the best we could as follows:

Beware of respectable people. Don't be afraid of your dreams. Remember all original work is laughed at to begin with. And the time will never come when man's fate on the earth will not be mostly concentrated in the word: Struggle!

Also it was said long ago that silence is a gift.

And after we had sent away this message we had a feeling that we had said too much and what we said could have been better put. The first part might better have read: Beware of respectable people; beware of crooks, but of all crooks beware of the respectable; beware of snobs, and especially middle-class snobs; beware of people who are perfectly gram- matical; beware of culture hounds; beware of the people who let their thinking be done for them and don't know it.

war, and continuing migration from the South. If a Negro family managed to escape the ghetto and to remain in a white neighborhood despite threats and pressure, the whites would move away. Vulpine real estate dealers preyed on both factions to profiteer in property sales and leasing.

Sandburg quoted a Harvard-educated Negro city bridge engineer on the crisis:

> "White citizens must be educated out of all hysteria over actual or prospective arrival of colored neighbors. All colored citizens do not make bad neighbors, although in some cases they will not make good ones. It is of the greatest importance, however, both to white and colored people, that the real estate dealers should cease to make a business out of commercializing racial antagonisms."

Sandburg prophesied that the Negroes would not stand for segregated standards forever and that there would be violence in their drive for equality. His articles were collected into a book, *The Chicago Race Riots, July, 1919,* and published by the newly established publishing house Harcourt, Brace and Howe, with a foreword by another prominent liberal, Walter Lippmann.

In the closing chapter, Sandburg concluded bluntly: "The race question is national and federal. No city or state can solve it alone. There must be cooperation between states. And there must be federal handling of it." This realization, of course, was to occur to others, but nothing was done toward achieving any tangible results until the Negro crusade of the fifties.

While Sandburg was in Sweden for the N.E.A., Henry Holt published his second volume of poetry, *Cornhuskers.* In his earlier poems Sandburg had written mostly about the city. Now, in the new poems, he was more concerned with the prairie and the American landscape, but the vein of social protest still ran strongly through the volume. The *Review of Reviews* said that Sandburg's poetry had the same "vitality and strength of the English tongue as it had in its beginnings." O. W. Firkins, who did not appreciate Sandburg (and never would), said that the only difference between Sandburg's two volumes of poetry was the difference "between black smoke and blue." Poet Louis Untermeyer praised Sandburg's use of the commonplace, common language, and slang.

That year, 1918, Carl Sandburg and Margaret Widdemer shared First Prize from the Poetry Society of America.

7

In Search of Lincoln

DURING his newspaper years, when he was becoming known as a daring new poet, Sandburg never relaxed the pursuit of his other interests. He continued lecturing for the J. B. Pond Lyceum Bureau and sometimes appeared on programs with poet Lew Sarett, whose lyrical evocations of American Indian life Sandburg had encouraged Harriet Monroe to publish. Now that Sandburg could be billed as a well-known poet, his speaking engagements multiplied, taking him to rich lodes of Lincoln lore. He added these to the books, clippings, and notes he had been amassing for years about the idol of his Galesburg years.

In these little towns Sandburg questioned his hosts about local people or libraries that might hold untapped Lincoln knowledge. When he found virgin material, he mined it to enrich his hoard of biographical data. He also continued to collect folk songs, another love that endured through all his years. No day was ever complete for Sandburg without a singing session with his favorite guitar of the moment.

In 1920, Louis Untermeyer wrote to Sandburg. He was looking for poems for an anthology of verse about Lincoln, and Sandburg contributed "Fire-Logs." He wrote to Untermeyer, "I aim to write a trilogy about Lincoln one day, to break down all this sentimentalizing about him. It's curious the company Lincoln keeps these days. I find his picture on the walls of politicians and big businessmen who do not understand him and probably would not approve of him if they did."

The J. B. Pond Lyceum Bureau

Presents

Carl Sandburg

"The Poet of the City"

Author of

"CHICAGO POEMS"
"CORNHUSKERS"
Etc.

and

Lew Sarett

LONE CARIBOU

"The Poet of the Wilderness"

Author of

"MANY, MANY MOONS," Etc.

in

A JOINT LECTURE
AND RECITAL

From Their Own Writings

*Americans All in an
All American Program*

Managed by

J. B. POND LYCEUM BUREAU

50 East 42nd Street   -   -   New York
Fine Arts Building   -   -   Chicago

1920 Sandburg-Sarett tour.

CARL SANDBURG

Lecture - recital: readings from his books, "Chicago Poems," "Cornhuskers," "Smoke and Steel."

Bookings of Mr. Sandburg for platform engagements, address:

Mitchell Dawson,
First National Bank Bldg., Chicago

AUTUMN BOOK LIST ANNOUNCEMENT

Smoke and Steel

By CARL SANDBURG, author of "Chicago Poems" and "Cornhuskers."

A book of underworlds and overtones, by the most American of American poets. In it the commonplace of everyday life—a street corner, the glare of the furnace or the whirr of machinery, a man in shirt sleeves, a girl cashier in a restaurant—are transformed and fused into the eternal warp and woof of life. The glow, the humor, the crude power and passion of life are here; but over all there broods the spirit of warm desire and understanding that gives them a new meaning. American poetry, all too often in the past, has been graceful and anaemic; Carl Sandburg brings it a virile "roughneck" power. It has been "literary"; he brings it the current coinage of American speech. It has been cold; he brings it a warm, mystical tenderness. To some of us he seems the chief spokesman of the world's dreams today.

HARCOURT, BRACE & HOWE
1 W. 47th St., New York

On the Dawson circuit. Sandburg was booked through the early 1920's by Mitchell Dawson, as well as by the J. B. Pond Lyceum Bureau.

That October, Sandburg's third volume of verse, *Smoke and Steel*, was published. A mixture of urban and country verse, it was dedicated to Sandburg's brother-in-law, Edward Steichen. (Sandburg's *Chicago Poems* had been dedicated to his wife, Paula, and his second volume of poetry, to his daughters, Margaret and Janet.)

As usual, *The Dial* attacked. Arthur Wilson wrote that the new poetry shared "the sententious garrulity which makes nine-tenths of Whitman impossible to any man of taste." Young Edmund Wilson, who was one day to become an authority in American letters, cited Sandburg in an article in *Vanity Fair* as an example of how the Industrial Revolution was blunting the sensitivities of American poets.

But elsewhere *Smoke and Steel* was met with enthusiasm, along with some reservations. Sandburg was becoming too much the mystic, some said. He was verbose, redundant in theme and language, according to others. Amy Lowell wished that he would stop writing about the people. The mob was vulgar, she said, and offered no contrasts. The London *Times Literary Supplement* said he raised current mediocrity above past glories in his quest for the timely. Untermeyer contrasted the styles of the nation's leading poets, Robert Frost and Sandburg: Frost never exhausted the limited milieu of his poetry, whereas Sandburg, in his hunger for new experience, devoured the world and its people.

Sandburg told Walter Yust in an interview for *The Bookman* that what he and his *compères* were trying to achieve was " a kind of freedom." He said, resorting to a folk axiom he had cited twenty years before in one of his Asgard Press volumes, "I guess really we don't know where we're going, but we're on our way. We may never win this freedom; maybe we'll be interesting to future generations only because we are a step toward a higher development. I don't know."

The year before, in 1919, the Sandburgs had moved to Elmhurst (Maywood had become overpopulated for a man who valued peace and privacy). They had moved into a rambling frame structure that Sandburg called Happiness House. Here the Sandburg's entertained their friends, (Sandburg formed many—and lasting—friendships, some extending as long as eighty years.) Harcourt recalled that he had met, in a visit to Happiness House, the ailing radical organizer Eugene Debs, who was recuperating in a nearby sanitarium. Debs had served part of a commuted ten-year sentence, for violation of the Espionage

Act, something he had done to express his opposition to the American war effort. Harcourt wrote:

> Debs had been teaching some of the songs he had heard his fellow prisoners sing. I had come to talk to Carl about publishing some of the stories he was telling his children, and I did get the manuscript of his "Rootabaga Stories" from him as a result of that visit, but the way he and Debs sang the "Sam Hall" song haunted me, and I put away the thought of those prison songs for future use.

In 1920, Sandburg initiated something that became one of his trademarks. He was speaking at Cornell University, his first campus engagement. At the end of his talk he took out his guitar and said, "I will now sing a few folk songs that somehow tie into the folk quality I have tried to get into my verse. They are all authentic songs people have sung for years. If you don't care for them and want to leave the hall, it will be all right with me. I'll only be doing what I'd be doing if I were at home, anyway." The audience loved the songs, and folk singing became a beloved feature of Sandburg's platform appearances.

Traveling the trains on the lecture circuit, Sandburg often passed the time in the smoking car with traveling salesmen and business executives. He was constantly being asked what his line was, and when

Happiness House. The Carl Sandburgs lived in Elmhurst, Illinois, from 1919 to 1928.

With Helga (left) and Janet (right).

he answered, "Poetry," he succeeded in drawing laughter from everyone. Finally, because his real line was not taken seriously, he began to reply, "I'm chairman of the board and president of the North American Pawpaw Growers Association." That satisfied them. It had a banal ring they could accept.

Another *Daily News* reporter who was a frequent visitor at the Sandburgs was Lloyd Lewis, who always came with his lovely wife, Kathryn. The two writers were close friends, and they shared an ardor for Civil War research. Lewis was later to write excellent biographies of Ulysses S. Grant and William Tecumseh Sherman.

In 1922, Eugene Debs wrote to a friend, David Karsner, about how much his visits with Sandburg meant to him. "He [Sandburg] lives only three blocks from here and I shall have his three little household gods [the Sandburg daughters, now including Helga, who was born in 1920] for playmates and that will be the most vital part of my restorative treatment. . . . Last night I was with Carl Sandburg and Sinclair Lewis at the Sandburg home till midnight and then that beautiful brace brought me home. It was a wonderful occasion—an event in our lives. . . . Carl came with his guitar Saturday evening and gave the patients here a most charming entertainment in folklore. It was a complete conquest and they all love him. Lewis will also entertain them. . . ."

In later years, when he was governor of Illinois, Adlai Stevenson spoke of Sandburg's visits to Adlai's father, Lewis Green Stevenson. One occasion he never forgot was the time Sandburg and Lewis Stevenson went off to see the former governor of Illinois, Joseph W. Fifer (who liked to be called Private Joe because of his rank in the Civil War), with a bottle of rare bourbon to loosen Fifer's tongue for war reminiscences. Years later Stevenson wrote:

> Armed with whiskey, Carl and my father set forth for Gov. Fifer's, confident that it would stir his recollections and assured that he would share it with them. Sight of the whiskey added to the warmth of Fifer's greeting, but when father presented him with the bottle, he placed it, uncorked, on his desk, where father and Sandburg cast frustrated glances at it throughout the interview.
>
> My acquaintance with Carl Sandburg extends through many years. Among my most pleasant recollections are parties in Chicago in the Twenties and Thirties where I listened to him sing from his songbag to the inimitable accompaniment of his guitar, and happy evenings with him and the late Lloyd Lewis, where anecdotes, Lincoln and music took us far into the night.

Slabs of the Sunburnt West was dedicated in 1922 to the Sandburg's third daughter and last child, Helga. Malcolm Cowley wrote a friendly review for *The Dial,* which ran in the issue with T. S. Eliot's *The Waste Land*—a work that was appearing in print for the first time. Sandburg, said Cowley, "never wrote an American dictionary"—as H. L. Mencken had done with *The American Language*—but "he does something more hazardous and exciting: he writes American." In the *New Republic,* Raymond Holden admired Sandburg's "personality, genius, perspicacity, fire, love of life" but felt that his "vernacular beauty [was] often effaced by his fear that dignity will estrange it." And the reviewer for *The New York Times* cautioned Sandburg against becoming "the Professional Chanter of Virility."

The same year Harcourt, Brace and Company published Sandburg's collection of children's tales, *Rootabaga Stories,* to critical acclaim. Sandburg wrote in its Preface: "I wanted something more in the American lingo. I was tired of princes and princesses and I sought the American equivalent of elves and gnomes. I knew that American children would respond, so I wrote some nonsense tales with American fooling in them."

Sandburg was working hard. He had written five books in six years—these in addition to his newspaper work, lectures, and readings. He continued to live simply, as he did all his life—eating cheap lunches and walking long distances to save streetcar fares and dressing in plain, sturdy clothing. Money worries were never far from his mind. It was the product, not only of an impoverished childhood and of the times he had been without a job as a younger man, but also of his fears for the security of his children. Margaret, the eldest, suffered from epilepsy, and Janet, although Sandburg did not know this then, was to be struck by a car and seriously injured in 1929. Helga was still a small child, and although he again had no way of foreseeing this, Margaret and Janet were to remain in their parents' home for years to come.

Early in 1923, on the eve of the publication of another volume of children's tales, *Rootabaga Pigeons,* Sandburg went to New York to discuss his next book with Harcourt. Harcourt was aware of his author's lifelong interest in Lincoln and suggested that Sandburg attempt a "life of Lincoln for teen-age boys and girls." Sandburg agreed to write a Lincoln biography for young adults, and he told Harcourt how he had first begun to admire Lincoln when he himself was a young boy and passed the Lincoln-Douglas debate plaque on the milk route every morning. Harcourt later remembered that discussion and Sandburg's remarks about how that plaque had influenced his thoughts:

> It led him to read the entire series of debates and then on to other material connected with Lincoln. As he talked, he referred a number of times to the idea I had suggested and finally asked, "a volume of 400 pages?" "Yes," I said, "but it might run to a little longer." When he left me, he had agreed to try his hand at what we described as a "boy's life of Lincoln."

Immediately after his return to Elmhurst, Carl began to sort, assemble, and assess the Lincoln material he had been collecting for

TOP LEFT *In a favorite chair.*

MIDDLE *Fellow newspaperman, Lloyd Lewis, a frequent visitor to Happiness House, enjoys a Sandburg quip.*

BOTTOM LEFT *Paula and Carl in their garden, 1925.*

ABOVE *Carl Sandburg, age forty-eight, with his youngest daughter, Helga, age five, at Happiness House, 1926.*

years. He later compared this task to sorting oranges. He was the patient sifter of what was "humanly interesting" and what was only useless detail. He described the work later: "I found myself not guiding, but being guided by, the material." Many times his fascination with the job kept him working through the night.

From his letters to Lloyd Lewis and from remarks he had been making to friends for years, it is plain that Sandburg had been thinking for a long time about attempting a definitive Lincoln biography—not simply a young people's Lincoln. "The Lincoln drags," he wrote Lewis, "at least a dozen chapters have to be entirely rewritten, early ones where my ignorance was stupendous and will still be there in degree when the job is done."

Like prospectors working the same lode, the two men often swapped facts and sources of information. "If among your forthcoming scalawags you are to do Cash Clay or John H. Morgan," Sandburg wrote to Lewis, "you will find William H. Townsend at Lexington, Ky., had some original material. As I recall it he had learned that Morgan liked women and once took a bad wound because of delaying with one when he could have made his getaway."

In 1925, Sandburg went to New York to deliver his manuscript to Harcourt. Later Harcourt remembered: "That boy's life of Lincoln had grown into two volumes. . . . There was no title. At this time, Van Wyck Brooks had the office next to mine, and was acting informally for us as a special adviser. He was deeply moved by the work, and suggested the perfect title, 'Abraham Lincoln: The Prairie Years.'"

Later Sandburg told another version of how his Lincoln biography got its title. He was torn between two possible titles: *The Prairie Lincoln* and the ultimate choice. Sherwood Anderson dropped by the *Daily News* one night when Sandburg was working late on a movie review, and Sandburg asked him for his opinion. Anderson favored *The Prairie Lincoln*, but Sandburg and Lloyd Lewis preferred *Abraham Lincoln: The Prairie Years*, and this was the title under which the volume was published.

The *Pictorial Review* offered Harcourt $3,500 for serialization of excerpts from the book. "I told them I was convinced that 'The Prairie Years' was going to rank as one of the greatest biographies in the English language," Harcourt wrote of the incident, "and that I couldn't consider anything less than thirty-thousand dollars. They gasped, but were convinced in the end."

Sinclair Lewis and wife Grace Livingstone Hegger Lewis. In 1922 Lewis wrote to his wife, "It's been a great week. . . . I've been Union Laboring hard. Most important, two evenings at Carl Sandburg's home, out (at) Elmhurst, with Gene Debs. . . ."

Carl Sandburg

Sandburg was on a tour of Texas, giving lectures and readings, and Harcourt's telegram with news of the sale just missed him at Waco. A professor located the poet at Commerce, Texas, and sent him a wire reading: "I have received the following telegram. Does it mean anything to you?" He then quoted the Harcourt message. Sandburg replied, "Thank you for sending me a telegram with news equivalent to falling heir to a farm."

This was the first large sum of money Sandburg had earned from his writing, and when he returned home with the news, he and his wife wept with joy. It meant the end of their anxiety over the security of their daughters.

Sandburg's biography begins in 1776. It traces Lincoln's ancestors back to Virginia and follows his people westward to Kentucky, Indiana, and, finally, to Illinois. It takes Abraham Lincoln's life from childhood in Springfield to inauguration as President of the United States in Washington. A 900-page two-volume study, it was published in February, 1926, on the one hundred and seventeenth anniversary of Lincoln's birth.

Throughout the world the book was acclaimed almost unani-

Helga (left) and Margaret Sandburg (right), with Dr. Jim Freese's daughter in the middle, enjoy a swim.

LEFT *Dr. Arthur W. "Jim" Freese (left) and Sandburg feigning drunkenness as a joke, for Mrs. Freese's photo album (circa 1928).*

ABOVE *Jim Freese and Carl Sandburg, in 1960, share a joke over the "good old days."*

mously as a classic and a great work. H. L. Mencken called it, with his typical decisiveness, "the best American biography." The reviewer for the London *Times Literary Supplement* wrote, "It says much for Mr. Sandburg's clarity of thought and expression that he makes us see American politics almost intelligibly. Again and again we watch Lincoln bring forth his meditations to the light through great struggle."

In later years, Dr. Paul M. Angle, noted Lincoln scholar and author of *A Shelf of Lincoln Books*, supported earlier verdicts of the work by saying that it "stands alone. . . . If the word 'incomparable' be given its literal meaning, only this book among the thousands which deal with the life of Lincoln deserves it."

There were factual errors in Sandburg's great work, as a number of Lincoln authorities were eager to point out. The most serious of them, which Sandburg later admitted and corrected in subsequent editions of the work, was the author's acceptance of some spurious letters as proof of a romance between Lincoln and Ann Rutledge in the New Salem days—a favorite legend that, Sandburg conceded, he had wished to believe because it had seemed in character for young Lincoln.

111

But what Sandburg had done better than any biographer had ever done before was to create a picture of Abraham Lincoln the man, set against the context of his times. In *The Prairie Years*, Lincoln stepped down from the pedestal where generations of hero-worshipers had placed him and became a warm- (sometimes hot-) blooded human being—a good-humored man capable of anger, a devoted public servant who was nevertheless a shrewd politician who would seize the main chance. Above all, Abraham Lincoln became a man with failings, but a man who was somehow able to employ his weaknesses in noble pursuits.

Sandburg had not neglected the Lincoln lore, for true or not, it had become part of the background against which Americans knew the man. And Sandburg drew upon his own experience of life on the Illinois prairie—with its folk humor and native wit—to create a Lincoln who was truly a product of that homely background.

With his Lincoln biography, Sandburg became a beloved celebrity and remained one throughout his life. With fame came the first taste of riches. With royalties, the Sandburgs bought a summer house on a seven-acre plot of sand dunes on the shore of Lake Michigan near Harbert, Michigan. Carl was to keep his job at the *Daily News*, which was paying him $75 a week, for another six years. It was not a large salary for a poet and biographer of his increasing renown; but the job was not too much of a drain on his time or his great energy, and to a man who had known want, it meant security.

That autumn Sandburg's *Selected Poems* was published. The Introduction by the British novelist and critic Rebecca West served to spread his reputation abroad. "He can describe the inner life of the strong young men who wander about the vast land, proud and yet perplexed," she wrote, "proud because they are lending their strength to the purposes of the new civilization, perplexed because they do not know what it is all about." Sandburg, she added, "expresses the whole life of the Middle West of to-day."

That winter, when Sandburg was in Santa Fe, New Mexico, for a reading, his brother Martin sent him a telegram to notify him of the death of their mother. Clara had died on December 30, in her seventy-seventh year. She had died easily, leaving behind a testament of courage in eloquent, if broken, English for her children. And she had lived long enough to see her restless son—the one she and her husband, August, had worried about—attain deserved fame. Sandburg had dedicated the biography to his parents as "Workers of the Illinois Prairie."

In 1927, Sandburg's long years of collecting the folk songs of America resulted in the publication of *The American Songbag*—a landmark work in this field. Of its 280 songs, more than 100 had been collected by Sandburg in his years of ranging the land and had not been published before. Because Sandburg had never studied musical notation, the arrangements had been made for him by a variety of musically trained friends.

The songs reflected almost every aspect of the American experience, from Colonial days to World War I. There were songs and ballads of the American Revolution and the Civil War, of immigrants and frontier days, of sailors and cowboys and miners and factory workers, stevedores and slaves and chain gangs, hoboes and Wobblies.

Although many of them were attributed to little-known men and women whom Sandburg had met in his travels, quite a few of them had been learned from famous people. In the introduction to each song, Sandburg explained where he had learned it. Of "Hallelujah, I'm a Bum" he wrote: "This old song heard at the water tanks of railroads in Kansas in 1897 and from harvest hands who worked in the wheat fields of Pawnee County." Other songs were attributed to "Red [Sinclair] Lewis of Sauk Center, Minnesota" ("A Horse Named Bill"); "Lloyd Lewis, Free Quaker, and former and early resident of Pendleton, Indiana, a man of sterling integrity and many devices" ("Where O Where Is Old Elijah?"); and Robert Frost, who "learned as a boy on the wharves of San Francisco" the lusty ballad "Whisky Johnny."

The American Songbag confirmed Sandburg's right to be ranked as one of the pioneering collectors in American folklore. Only two other men had done as much as he had done in American folk music at that time: Cecil Sharp, the English scholar, had traced the lineage of the American folk ballads and songs of the Southern mountains to their Anglo-Saxon sources, and John Lomax had saved many of the ethnic songs of America from extinction. It was a natural interest for Sandburg, who realized, as so much of his poetry demonstrated, that in the songs and sayings of a people there is truth—an expression of the national character and wisdom at its most common level.

As Sandburg grew famous, the Hearst empire made another effort to lure him into its fold. Hearst offered Sandburg $30,000 a year to write a column for the newspaper chain, but Sandburg's earlier experience had convinced him that it was beyond his power to do business

with Hearst and at the same time maintain his integrity. He rejected the offer.

In 1928 the first twenty-six chapters of *The Prairie Years,* dealing with Lincoln's youth, were published as *Abe Lincoln Grows Up* for younger readers. Another volume of verse, *Good Morning, America,* was also published. It was warmly reviewed by Horace Gregory, Babette Deutsch, and other critics. Leon Whipple in *The Survey* called it "a paean to this gorgeous shield of American earth," and Mark Van Doren wrote that Sandburg "knows better than any of his contemporaries how to put a flowing world on paper." As usual, there were dissenters. Edwin Seaver in the *New Republic* said the volume was weaker than Sandburg's earlier works, and Percy Hutchinson said in *The New York Times Book Review* that he thought Sandburg was parochial, formless, and lacking in subtlety.

Sandburg had reached another turning point in his life. He had to decide what to do next. But it really was not a very difficult choice. While he was writing *Abraham Lincoln: The Prairie Years,* he believed that he would be able to complete the picture of Lincoln as the wartime President in a three- or four-chapter prologue or perhaps in an epilogue. Sandburg later remarked of this belief: "There was valor in my innocence!"

His "prairie years" were over.

8

Lincoln's Homer

SANDBURG's life up to his fiftieth year, which came in 1928, was the ideal preparation for what would be his greatest prose effort—his portrait of Abraham Lincoln as Civil War President. In moving from Lincoln the public figure to Lincoln the man beneath, Sandburg was able to draw on a wealth of personal experience.

There had been, for Sandburg, the lean years as the son of poor immigrants on the Illinois prairie. There had been an adolescence spent among people who spoke of Lincoln as a lost friend and colleague, and there had been the vagabond years, in which the writer had been exposed to an incurable contagion of enthusiasm for democracy. During his Socialist years Sandburg had learned the realities of politics and the necessity of forging between candidate and constituency a bond of sympathy that would serve as a bridge on which the needs and desires of the people could be carried to their lawmakers. From this background Carl Sandburg grew to apotheosize the "People" (a name he always capitalized) as an ineluctable force for good.

His newspaper years had taught him research and organization. His lectures and readings had enabled him to crisscross the land, where he exhausted every source of Lincoln and Civil War materials he found. The friendships he formed as a renowned poet and biographer of Lincoln's early life had opened to him the inestimable resources of private Civil War collections. The lawyer Oliver Barrett owned an

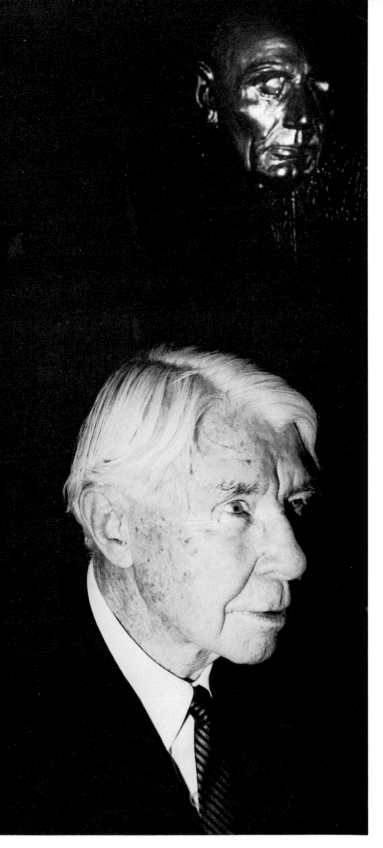

Lincoln's Homer.

incomparable one, and Frederick Hill Meserve possessed an un-paralleled collection of photographs of the Lincoln era.

And Sandburg was possessed with boundless energy and curiosity. When his job with the *Daily News* kept him in Chicago, Carl's friends were amused to see the famous poet crouched on the sidewalk beside an outdoor stand of a used-books store, perusing old magazines, seeking the rare fact or reminiscence on some aspect of Lincoln's years that may not have been recorded anywhere else. Had it not been for Sandburg's perseverance, these might have been forever lost to historians.

Now, at the age of fifty, Sandburg finally had the time, the financial security, and the self-assurance to permit himself the luxury of attempting his "epilogue" to *The Prairie Years*.

That year Mrs. Sandburg began to convert the spacious many-windowed white-frame house on the dunes overlooking the lake into a year-round residence. When the family moved there permanently four years later, it provided Sandburg with the privacy and the peace he needed, as well as the space for his ingenious research and filing system. There he re-created the turbulent wartime years of Lincoln.

In 1929, Janet was struck by a car in front of Three Oaks High School in Harbert. She was unconscious for several days, and it was many months before she could return to school.

The following year Sandburg published more children's stories and a selection of his verse suitable for children, entitled *Early Moon*. By this time his assignment at the *News* had been reduced to a regular column headed "A Few Pages from His Notebook" under a byline, "By Carl Sandburg," that was larger than the title. But a large byline could not serve to keep Carl Sandburg at the newspaper forever. He had become so immersed in his Lincoln work and so successful with his outside writings that in 1932 he quit the *News* at last and moved to the renovated home at Harbert.

It was a plain house of homely exterior. (The Sandburgs never seemed to worry about appearances.) But inside, the uncurtained windows provided sunshine and warmth. Bookcases were everywhere. An attic room was fitted out as Carl's workroom. It had a wood-burning stove, a cot, and deal bookcases. In lieu of a desk, Sandburg placed his typewriter on a wooden crate. It was just the right height, and it was stable. Carl enjoyed thinking that if Grant had been able to conduct his war from a cracker barrel, he, Carl Sandburg, could write

LEFT *The Lincoln collector (Oliver Barrett) and the Lincoln writer (Carl Sandburg) on a Harbert bridge in the 1930's.*

RIGHT *Chikaming Goat Farm—the sand dune residence of the Sandburgs from 1928 to 1945.*

about it with the same lack of luxury. Outside the attic was a spacious sun deck, where he wrote on clear warm days from late spring to early autumn.

In his first two years of research Sandburg burrowed through more than 1,000 books for the source material he needed. He marked the passages he wanted copied and passed the books either to his wife, his daughters, or a secretary. (At times he had two secretaries working at typewriters on the glassed-in porch of the house that over-looked the lake.) Years later Sandburg recalled with nostalgia how his girls had helped him with his big work: "I can still hear the girls beg-ging, 'Oh, Dad, it's such a nice day out! Do we have to classify today?' "

Before Sandburg had completed his task, 4,000 volumes on Lin-coln or some aspect of his times had passed through Sandburg's mill. Some were gutted of the material he wanted, and the relevant pages were absorbed into growing files in a system that no one but Carl un-derstood completely. (Or so he thought, for often it was Paula who located in the files some "lost" data her husband needed.) There was an envelope for every major subject Sandburg hoped to cover—"Looks," "Laughter," "Religion," "The Gettysburg Address"—envelopes which became chapters as long as or longer than an average sized book.

The house was filled with books—books on shelves, books in stacks. A second-floor room became the Lincoln Room, and as books were drained from it (with perhaps part of their substance absorbed by the growing files), they were passed on to be stored in the barn.

Carl Sandburg appears very Lincolnesque at the edge of the sandblow where he and Paula planted young poplars to hold the sand between the evergreens.

Helga milks a Toggenburg at Chikaming Goat Farm, 1935.

After a swim, Carl and Paula watch Lake Michigan's shimmering water meet the sky, 1930.

Carl Sandburg, age fifty-two, on the beach, 1930.

Helga, Janet, and Margaret with their parents near Harbert, Michigan, in 1930.

Helga, Edward Steichen, Sandburg's police dog, Carl Sandburg, and Janet at the dunes near their home in Michigan in 1930.

In his thoroughness, Sandburg pored through all the bound volumes of the *Congressional Globe* of the Civil War era, as well as through all 133 volumes of the *Official Records of the Rebellion*. He spent months studying these compilations alone.

From late fall until early spring Sandburg still followed the lyceum circuit. He read poetry, lectured, and sang folk songs in halls and campuses as distant as the University of Hawaii. Often he traveled to colleges and universities to accept honorary degrees that were conferred on him by the dozens. But it was the location of the school, rather than anything else, that determined whether Carl Sandburg would accept an invitation. He went wherever there was still some Lincoln or Civil War data to be collected.

His friends continued to visit him, although he had less time to devote to social amenities. There were memorable songfests with Lloyd and Kathryn Lewis, Adlai Stevenson, and Sinclair Lewis. And there was time every day (Sandburg made time) to sing for the pleasure of himself and his family and to create more American fairy tales for his growing daughters.

His temper was not always even. On days when the work was moving with difficulty, his daughters had to move quietly through the house because "papa is working." If he was disturbed too often, he could come raging from his loft to wield his baritone in outraged scoldings over the interruption of his work. He was human.

Carl Sandburg had come late in life to his major work, and it was to occupy him for a dozen years. But as he said after the labor was finished, he had come to this difficult effort at the proper time in his career: "Between forty and fifty I would have had more drive, but less perspective, less understanding, less wisdom, and less experience. But had I waited until I was sixty, I would not have had the physical endurance to finish the job."

Sometimes he had to interrupt his major task for a labor of love or for an occasional spin-off from the big book with which to support the family throughout those years. One such work was *Mary Lincoln: Wife and Widow*, for which historian Paul M. Angle provided the documentation of the relevant correspondence. It was a sentimental look at the controversial life of Mrs. Lincoln, a tragic life which some other historians treated less kindly. Sandburg wrote of her as a woman who had "lived, suffered, laughed, wept, sat in candlelight and shadows, and passed out from the light of the living sun." It was a

Carl Sandburg, age fifty-four, has quit the News *and joined his family at Harbert, Michigan, 1932.*

*Martin Godfrey Sand-
burg (1880–1944), age
fifty-two, became an
executive at Rath
Packing Company in
Galesburg, Illinois.
He sponsored the
company baseball
team.*

minor pause of no great significance except to other Lincoln scholars.

Mrs. Sandburg, an erudite, energetic woman, could not occupy all her time as a housewife and an aide to her husband. So the Sandburgs began to raise registered goats on their seven-acre holding, which they began to call Chikaming Goat Farm. Paula Sandburg became an authority on the care and breeding of pedigreed goats, and in succeeding years she won many honors for the quality of her herd. The Sandburgs became devoted to goat's milk and cheese, although their visitors did not always share their enthusiasm for it.

Lloyd Lewis' biography of William Tecumseh Sherman, *Sherman: Fighting Prophet,* was published in 1932, and Sandburg wrote a foreword for the book. Good friends through their newspaper years, the two writers were drawn even closer by their shared interest in the Civil War. Sometimes, perhaps playfully, Sandburg tried to lure Lewis away from his contemplated biography of Ulysses S. Grant's early years (published thirty years later, posthumously, as *Captain Sam Grant*) into another field of research.

On the Matson liner Malolo, Carl and Paula return from Hawaii, where Carl had given a series of lectures, 1934.

Helga Sandburg, who would later become a writer in her own right, with her parents and a herd of Nubians, 1938.

April 6, 1937.

My dear Mr. Sandburg:-

      Your letter has at last reached my desk and I am, indeed, grateful to you. I have long wanted to talk with you about Lincoln - and many other things - so if at any time you are coming to Washington I hope you will let me know beforehand and come in to see me.

      You have reconstructed so well the picture of the executive duties and life in Lincoln's day that perhaps you will be interested in seeing at least the same relative problems at first-hand in these days.

      Very sincerely yours,

Franklin D Roosevelt

Carl Sandburg, Esq.,
Harbert,
Michigan.

Sculptor Jo Davidson does a head of Sandburg in 1939—the year The War Years *came out.*

Paul M. Angle, former director of the Chicago Historical Society, collaborated with Sandburg on Mary Lincoln: Wife and Widow *(1932).*

You will do an immemorial Grant. . . [Sandburg wrote to Lewis in a letter in these years]. Perhaps that will yet lead on into a Jefferson. . . . For a great Grant biography, I have merely a normal appetite. For a 2, 3, 4-vol. Jefferson I have depths of hunger. . . . The Jefferson work is a dream and a prayer.

In a later letter Sandburg continued:

Jefferson is the only other President of the USA I can think of who would draw out of me the same drudgery, and sustain me thru it, as Lincoln does. He was a poet, artist, dreamer, son ofagun, hellraiser, redheaded fiddler, farmer, inventor, politician. . . . In all my delvings and ramblings around in Jefferson material, the pull has always been strong toward him, the lacks and cheapnesses so few, the high spots and fine points so many and lovable.

In 1936, Sandburg published his most ambitious volume of poetry, his longest work, *The People, Yes,* which was enriched by his years of collecting folk songs and sayings, humor and wisdom of the "People."

130

It was almost an anthology of folklore, woven together by passages of Sandburgian free verse. He called this long, loosely organized poem his "footnote to the last words of the Gettysburg address."

Published in the depths of the Depression and proclaiming the ultimate triumph of the "People" through their ability to endure hardships, *The People, Yes* was a timely inspiration to America. It was the emphatic affirmation of Sandburg's belief in democracy:

> Man will never arrive, man will always be on the way.
> It is written he shall rest but never for long.
> The sea and the wind tell him he shall be lonely, meet love,
> be shaken with struggle, and go on wanting.

Sandburg and Oliver R. Barrett discuss Sandburg's Lincoln Collector: The Story of the Oliver R. Barrett Lincoln Collection *(1949).*

The work was well received, but there were a few critics who felt that it did not manifest a poetical development. Others branded its author as the eternal questioner of man's purpose, identity, and ultimate destiny—a questioner whose only answer was silence. It was a triumphant work, and much of the reason for it undoubtedly was that Sandburg was beginning to see in the New Deal program of Franklin D. Roosevelt the realization of his own efforts at social protest thirty years before.

The year before the publication of *The People, Yes,* Sandburg had been moved to write the President a long letter full of praise and encouragement. It read, in part:

> All the time you keep growing—so it seems to some of us who read you from a distance. In wide human outlook—in utterance and in silence—in an austerity that deepens from year to year—you seem as a Chief Magistrate almost too good to be true. . . . Having written for ten years now on "Abraham Lincoln: The War Years," starting this year on the fourth and final volume, I have my eyes and ears in two eras and cannot help drawing parallels. One runs to the effect that you are the best light of democracy that has occupied the White House since Lincoln. You have set in motion trends that to many are banners of dawn. . . .
>
> Your speeches like Lincoln's will stand the test of time. . . . What many of us have come to see is that you had long preparation for what you are doing—and as with Lincoln there has been a response of the People to you: they have done something to you and made you what you could not have been without them, this interplay operating steadily in your growth.

That year he had indeed begun the final volume of *The War Years,* but four years of endless revision and reorganization lay ahead of him. The deceptive ease and logic of his finished works were the result of unstinting labor.

Lloyd Lewis had encouraged Sandburg through all the long years of his work and had followed his friend's steady progress. In 1938, as Sandburg neared the end of his task, Lewis wrote to him with a suggestion of a symphony of words for culminating the tragic grandeur of the climax of *The War Years.* Sandburg replied:

> I should have mentioned that I shall watch these points to be corrected which you named in your letter, and you have thanks for them. And enclosed is a passage now planned to go at about the

Lincoln Memorial, Washington, D. C.

very end of the book trying to evaluate the hurricane and the central life of it. This may be followed by free verse meditation on dust and dream dust and how what is placed away under stone and brass in a tomb may nevertheless step out as a whitesmoke ghost to haunt the earth for long afterward.

When at last he had written his chapter on the assassination of Lincoln, "Blood on the Moon," Sandburg was shaken. He felt as if he had lived and suffered through Lincoln's wound and the nation's tragedy. "I was parting with him, after all those years, like people who had lived with him. When Lincoln died, for a time lights went out for me. The tears came. I do not know how a man could hold so many —and be unashamed as they ran down his cheeks an hour, two hours, more."

In the spring of 1939, Carl Sandburg went to New York City and delivered his manuscript (nearly 1,200,000 words) to Harcourt. Harcourt later recalled the event: "When Carl brought me the manuscript of the last four volumes, he said, 'This has grown into a scroll, a chronicle. There's one thing we can say for it: It is probably the only book ever written by a man whose father couldn't write his name, about a man whose mother couldn't write hers.'"

But the writer's work was not done. It was to take five months to prepare the manuscript for the printers, and Sandburg moved into the home of Isabel Ely Lord, an associate of Harcourt's, to prepare with her the final typescript, to write captions for photographs and other illustrations, and, finally, to read proofs as the massive work began to move through the printers.

On December 3, 1939, Carl Sandburg's work was published by Harcourt, Brace and Company in four volumes. They were priced at $20 a set. Each of the first three volumes ran to more than 650 pages, and the fourth was 413 pages—a total of more than 2,400 pages. It was longer than the writings of William Shakespeare, and it was longer than all the books of the Bible. When interviewers asked about this monumental creation, Sandburg said, "That son-of-a-gun Lincoln grows on you."

The day after publication, Sandburg was the cover subject of a *Time* Magazine portrait that combined his biography with a review of unstinting praise for *The War Years*. From everywhere came laudation for Sandburg's incredible achievement. Henry Steele Commager said of it: "The poets have always understood Lincoln, from Whitman to Emerson to Benet, and it is fitting that from the pen of a poet has come the greatest of all Lincoln biographies. One of the great biographies of our literature." Charles A. Beard wrote: "When the specialists have finished scraping, refining, dissenting, and adding, I suspect that Mr. Sandburg's work will remain for long years to come a noble monument of American literature." Lloyd Lewis, who had lived with the work as long as Sandburg had, summarized the achievement in a sentence: "A great American democrat has come at last to his most sympathetic, and, at the same time, his most searchingly detailed portrait at the hands of another great American democrat." And playwright Robert E. Sherwood, author of *Abe Lincoln in Illinois* and other notable historical dramas, termed it "a mighty summation" and said, "It is so great a work that it will require great reading and great reflection before any true appreciation of its permanent value can be formed."

Much later, after a proper interval of years in which to consider and weigh Sandburg's achievement, the talented historian Allan Nevins assessed *The War Years* as a "book homely but beautiful, learned but simple, exhaustively detailed but panoramic, it occupied a niche all

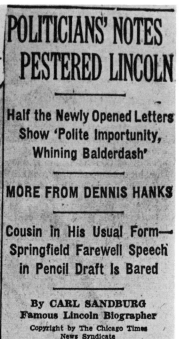

POLITICIANS' NOTES PESTERED LINCOLN

Half the Newly Opened Letters Show 'Polite Importunity, Whining Balderdash'

MORE FROM DENNIS HANKS

Cousin in His Usual Form— Springfield Farewell Speech in Pencil Draft Is Bared

By CARL SANDBURG
Famous Lincoln Biographer

WASHINGTON, July 28—What new in politics is often termed the gravy train was known in Lincoln's time as the hog trough and the proper petitions and improper shennanigans, wheedling, groaning and griping of it runs through about half of the letters in the papers newly opened to the public in the Library of Congress.

Among the groaners and gripers was former Congressman William Kellogg of Canton, Ill., and the latest revelation of his course of conduct is in a letter of April 8, 1863 from his home city. On the envelope in what seems to be the handwriting of the Secretary, John Hay, is a notation

A bitter letter from Hon. Wm. Kellogg Ill. declining the post of consul at Valparaiso

Below this in the handwriting of Lincoln is the comment:

I understand my friend Kellogg is ill-natured—therefore I do not read his letters.

A L

The species of polite importunity and whining balderdash that Lincoln had grown tired of hearing from Kellogg are in a sentence from the long-drawn letter, as follows:

"At the time I was indiscreet enough to indicate to Your Excellency a desire for an appointment to any office, for which, I was vain enough to believe I was qualified but from the position now offered I am forced to conclude, that Your Excellency held a decidedly different opinion from my own on the subject, or that my political status was such that the Administration would suffer by my appointment to an office of the grade of those held by Peck, Wilmot, Olin, Fisher, Swett, Ashby and Carter and many other recent appointments."

Sandburg in Ralph Newman's Abraham Lincoln Book Shop, Chicago, 1951.

Sandburg with Ralph Newman, 1951.

its own, unlike any other biography or history in the language. . . ."
He went on to say:

> The book indulges in none of that hero-worship which so
> marred Nicolay and Hay's ten-volume panegyric. It frankly disclosed
> Lincoln's want of organizing power, his uncouthness, his frequent
> mistakes of judgment, his bewilderment, his self-distrust ("I some-
> times think I am just an old fool," he told his son), his indecisions,
> his fits of gloom. But it also shows how steadfastly he strove against
> the problems that bethorned and quagmired his path, and which
> harried him to the melancholy verge of despair. It reveals the true
> magnitude of his labors from Sumter to Appomattox.
>
> In these twenty-five hundred pages, a distillation from a whole
> library, we have perhaps the best picture of a people in racked
> travail yet written by any pen. . . . For it is not merely a biography;
> it is a magnificent piece of history, a vital narrative of one of the most
> critical periods of the nation's life, and an epic story which for decades
> will hearten all believers in the virtues of democracy and the high
> potentialities of democratic leadership.

Sandburg told his friend Frederick Hill Meserve what he had
sought to achieve in his Lincoln biography. "Ignoramuses were talking
about Lincoln in a way that made me tired," Sandburg said. "The more
I got to love the companionship of this man the farther I went in my
job. 'The War Years' will take the people a week to read. Some will be
insulted. 'This is a bale of hay,' they will say, 'we want a ham sandwich.' Every now and then some pleasant human duffer will come up
to me and say, 'What would Lincoln do if he were here now?' I've written nearly two million words on the subject of Lincoln and they want
me to give them a convenient little capsule, possibly requiring two
swallows to get it down."

In the spring of 1940, Sandburg was awarded the Pulitzer Prize,
not for biography, but for history, a recognition of the breadth of his
achievement. It came as a fitting climax to the international acclaim
with which the great man had been lavished. Now for Sandburg, the
prairie years and the war years were over. As he had written of Abraham Lincoln:

And the night came with great quiet,
And there was rest.
The prairie years, the war years, were over.

136

dburg and the Rail
tter in Garfield Park
Chicago, 1957.

The Chicago Buddha.

9

Of the People

For Carl Sandburg, the great quiet would be a long time coming. In 1939, at sixty-one, an age when many men slow their pace and prepare for retirement, another quarter century of active years lay ahead of him. For Sandburg had become—and was to remain throughout his life—a beloved public figure. If his great work was behind him, there were other books—and other poetry—waiting to be written. The harvest years were over, but before him stretched a long mild winter in which to enjoy their fruits.

He was famous now, and Lloyd Lewis asked him if this might change his ideas about life. Despite his idealism, Sandburg was always a realist, and he replied, "I know a starving man who is fed never remembers all the pangs of his starvation. I know that."

Now, at last, the Civil War was ended, yet, he told an interviewer, there was still the "clearing away the scaffolding and the debris" to be done. But an even greater tragedy, World War II, had begun, and it would fill the mind of Sandburg as it did that of every other American for half a dozen terrible years. Not until it was finished did the world learn the stunning enormity of the Nazi insanity.

From the beginning Paula Sandburg felt that the United States had no choice but to ally itself with Great Britain and France if the Axis were to be defeated. Sandburg, however, was on the side of those who sought to keep America out of Europe's wars. Although he hoped that Britain and France would defeat Germany, he desired even more strongly that America would be able to avoid another war.

Perhaps this is why there was a serious, if stillborn, attempt by some prominent Republicans to induce Sandburg to become the GOP Presidential candidate in 1940. It was launched by a prominent Wall Street Republican, and those who became enthusiastic about the idea included Henry Luce, publisher of *Time* and *Life* magazines, and Geoffrey Parsons, editor of the New York *Herald Tribune*. Sandburg squelched the suggestion. It is difficult to understand how anyone could ever have thought that he would accept the Republican nomination. Although he had professed himself a political independent when he left the Socialist Party in 1917, Sandburg had allied himself publicly with the Roosevelt program throughout the thirties. When the campaign of 1940 began, Sandburg spoke at several large Democratic rallies for the reelection of Franklin Delano Roosevelt.

The President wrote to Sandburg that year to find out if the poet would consent to run for Congress against Clare Hoffman, the conservative Republican from the southwest district of Michigan, who was an arch-enemy of labor and the New Deal. "I have a real belief that you could win," Roosevelt wrote to Sandburg, "and it would be grand to have your kind of Lincoln liberal" in Congress. But Sandburg rejected the offer. He again turned his back on a political career in 1942, when Archibald MacLeish suggested to Roosevelt that Sandburg was the man to contest Hoffman's seat. (In 1948, Sandburg once more declined to become a candidate for political office—that time on the ticket of Henry Wallace's Progressive Party.)

In June, 1941, after France and half a dozen other free nations had fallen, Sandburg altered his stand on U. S. intervention in the war. At a Unity Day rally in the Chicago Stadium he shared the platform with Wendell Willkie (Republican Presidential candidate in 1940) to call for a unified nation. Excusing himself for "getting personal," Sandburg spoke out strongly against the isolationist, America First sympathies of Charles A. Lindbergh—a yesterday's hero gone sour. The speech received national attention. In it Sandburg said:

> It is a time when every American who prizes his citizenship is getting personal about it. He is asking himself where he stands, and he is asking his friends and neighbors where they stand, and he is asking some plain questions as to who is for America first and who isn't. . . .

140

When the war began in 1939 I was for the strictest of neutrality.
I hoped that France and Britain would in the end win the war. . . .

But France and Britain were not winning the war and Sandburg
had come to feel that American intervention was the world's only
hope. To Lindbergh's charge that the prointerventionists were "hysteri-
cal," Sandburg replied:

> Very well, then we are hysterical. Very well, then the Declaration
> of Independence is hysterical, the Constitution of the United States
> is hysterical, the Bill of Rights is hysterical, the Gettysburg Speech
> and the second inaugural of Abraham Lincoln are hysterical—and
> the men who fought and died to establish these documents and give
> them meaning, they were all hysterical. . . .
>
> Either way we go as a nation, there is going to be sacrifice and
> cost. I take the soothing babble of those who try to tell us that Hitler
> will let us alone as about the same thing the canary was saying to
> itself just before the cat swallowed it. . . .
>
> If we are going to be a self-determining nation of politically free
> people, deciding on our own way of life in line with the best tradi-
> tions of Jefferson and Lincoln, we are either going to throw in our
> help in Britain's fight now or at a later time we are going to have
> bitter regrets over what we might have done and failed to do.
>
> I am merely one of millions of watchers trying to read what
> will be the next twist of a wild and stupendous hurricane of fate. The
> future is beyond any man's reading. We are moving into an adventure
> beyond the horizon and I am taking my chances with those who say
> "God bless the President of the United States."

On the invitation of editor Richard Finnegan of the Chicago
Times, Sandburg returned to the newspaper business in 1941 to begin
a three-year stint as a weekly columnist for the Times Syndicate.
Finnegan felt that Sandburg's writings about the ordeal and triumph
of America might help inspire and unite the American people. In his
column Sandburg often wrote of the kinds of sacrifices Americans had
made to create their nation, and he called on his millions of readers
to support President Roosevelt in his battle with a grave threat to
freedom.

Sandburg was given the freedom to write about whatever interested him. He composed one column to express his sadness over the
suicide of Virginia Woolf:

In old clothes . . .

. . . or new . . .

. . . or with the great Segovia.

She walked out into the sea till she became a part of the river and the sea. She was tired of the land. And being tired of time, too, she turned her back on it and walked into a timeless beyond named eternity. . . . [Why she had done this] no one can tell. My reverence for her mind and heart goes on. She represented things money can not buy nor children be taught.

Frequently Sandburg ventured from the peace of his refuge at the lake to enjoy the attention he had earned. Often, too, reporters visited his weathered frame house atop the dunes to ask, on behalf of the public, how the old poet, bundled in layers of sweaters to keep out the damp, was faring.

When Sandburg was at home, he followed a quiet routine. He wrote late into the night and slept late into the morning. Then he opened the door of his attic study to get the breakfast tray his wife or one of his daughters had left for him. There was always a vacuum bottle full of hot coffee. Then he and Paula looked at their herd of pedigreed Nubian and Toggenburg goats and visited with neighbors to pass the time of day. Afternoons were for answering mail and writing the newspaper column. In the evenings, after dinner, the family gathered around the fireplace, sometimes with visiting friends, to talk or to read aloud. Almost every day the white-haired balladeer took his old guitar from the wall and sang songs of the American experience for his family and friends.

The Pulitzer Prize was the highest honor he had earned, but it was far from a singular honor. Honors and awards came to him in clusters. He was elected to the American Academy of Arts and Letters, given honorary doctorates in literature from Harvard, Yale, Syracuse, Dartmouth, Wesleyan, and a number of other universities. He was asked to deliver the Walgreen lecture series at the University of Chicago. For the Office of War Information, he wrote and narrated radio documentaries and government films to support the war effort.

In 1944, Sandburg had his first brush with Hollywood, and from this encounter he emerged neither winner nor loser. Metro-Goldwyn-Mayer hired Carl Sandburg for a reported $100,000 retainer to write a sweeping historical novel that would encompass the American dream from the *Mayflower* to World War II. Sandburg visited Hollywood to seal the pact, and the anecdotes that are told of his visit indicate that Hollywood could no more alter this aging rock of a man than he could change the fairy-tale city.

145

According to one story, Carl Sandburg remained silent and obviously unimpressed with all that he had seen on a guided tour through the movie studio. Finally, at lunch, his guide, at wit's end, made a last effort to impress Sandburg. "Would you believe it?" he said, gesturing toward a lovely actress in the dining room. "That gorgeous girl you just met is six feet two inches tall!" After mulling that over for a moment, Sandburg intoned, "Lincoln was six feet three and a half." Hollywood had met its match.

Sandburg labored for four years in his attempt to write the great American novel. But the book he wrote was neither a great American novel nor a screen spectacular.

When the war ended, the Sandburgs, nearing their seventies, were able to leave Michigan for a more temperate climate—a climate that would be better for them and that would provide a better grazing range for their goats. Mrs. Sandburg opted for North Carolina, known for its moderate climate and its lovely countryside, and Sandburg told her, "It was I who had picked the dunes, and now you shall pick the next place. I leave it entirely up to you."

She traveled to North Carolina to look for a new homesite and returned to tell him what she had found. It was a square white clapboard house with a portico and many windows (the Sandburgs loved the light). It had originally been built in 1833 for Christopher G. Memminger, later Secretary of the Treasury for the Confederacy under Jefferson Davis. They purchased the estate with its 240 acres of land, near Flat Rock, North Carolina, and named it Connemara.

In November, 1945, the Sandburgs crated their thousands of books, priceless papers, and personal belongings and shipped them with the goats to North Carolina. Wood was still in short supply because of the war, so they dismantled and shipped to their new home all their bookcases and shelves. The reporters from the Chicago newspapers came to record Sandburg's farewell to the Midwest, where he had spent nearly seventy years of his life. With his white cap worn low to shade his steely eyes, Sandburg spoke of his newspaper days in Chicago and of his years of work.

"I'm an old man, I'm taking life rather easy now," he said, explaining that he was writing at his novel only eight hours a day com-

FACING PAGE *Sandburg on the NBC radio program* Cavalcade of America *in Chicago in the early 1940's.*

Sandburg and Charlie Chaplin at the 1940 Democratic convention.

With his Japanese-American secretary, Miss Sanoa. During the war with Japan Sandburg hired another Japanese, Mr. Miyamto, to do the milking and goat herding. This was in an effort to show his trust in Japanese-Americans and to encourage others to help relocate them.

pared with the eighteen and twenty hours he had labored some days when he was working on Lincoln's biography. "I died when that book was finished. It's only my ghost that's leaving the Middle West. And I'll come back again and again, like a haunt, until I die again."

Walking along the lakeshore, he went on, "I love it here. I love to skip stones. I'm going to miss it all." And he would keep writing, he said. "I never let a day go by without doing some writing. You know, you've got to let the hook down and float a sinker to see what's doing in the old bean."

The dunes, in anything but summer, could be bleak and lonely. Connemara, however, had a gentle climate and was often warmed by sunlight. The farm on the lower slopes of Big Glassy Mountain ranged over rolling foothills, shaded by towering pines and oaks, with plenty of grassland for the goats. The restrained Colonial house was decorated to suit the Sandburgs, with white-painted walls and bookcases rising to the fifteen-foot ceilings in almost every room. The uncurtained high front windows of the bright, airy house overlooked the Blue Ridge

Carl Sandburg

Mountains, and Sandburg, sweeping his eyes over his vast estate, liked to announce to visitors, "Two hundred and forty acres! Ain't that a hell of a baronial estate for a proletarian poet!"

Every room in the house was supplied with a commercial-sized fire extinguisher—an understandable precaution for a man who had so much of his worldly treasure in books and papers. An upstairs room was fitted out as his workroom, and even when Sandburg began using a chrome and leather executive-style chair, the perennial orange crates were retained to serve as a typewriter desk and filing cabinets.

At the same time that the old mansion in North Carolina was being remodeled for the Sandburgs, restoration was under way of a dilapidated three-room workingman's shack in Galesburg, Illinois. It was 333 East Third Street on a dead-end street near the railroad tracks. Mrs. Adda Gentry George, widow of a Northwestern University professor, had settled in Galesburg to teach, and it was she who had decided that the birthplace of Carl Sandburg should be restored as a memorial to him. She formed the Carl Sandburg Association to raise funds with which to purchase the house from the Italian woman who owned it and to renovate it. The owner did not want her home turned into a Sandburg shrine, and she hid the plaque Mrs. George mounted beside the door and rolled away from her property a commemorative

Sandburg pays his respects at Lincoln's bier in Springfield, Illinois, February 12, 1961.

The Sandburg's donkey, Pico, grazes in front of Connemara.

Left to right: Mrs. Adda Gentry George (founder and honorary president of the Carl Sandburg Association), Sandburg, and Janet Greig Post (trustee of Knox College).

Mrs. Charles "Juanita" Bednar (president of the Carl Sandburg Association) and David Vilando (keeper of the cottage) stand in front of the Carl Sandburg birthplace (known as the Cottage), 1963.

boulder. But when the woman died, Mrs. George was able to buy the property from heirs, and the restoration began in December, 1945.

Mrs. George, at one point in her efforts, got Sandburg's sister, Mrs. Mary Johnson, to visit the little cottage in order to confirm that it really was Carl Sandburg's first home. At first Mrs. Johnson refused to admit that the drab shack was her birthplace and Carl's. Finally, after hedging all day, she said, "You're right, Adda, we were both born in this shack. I was just too ashamed to admit we were born in such a poor place."

It took ten months to complete the restoration. The cottage was filled with all that could be located of the furniture owned by the Sandburg family in the years of Carl's youth. There were other furnishings from that period to complete the setting. On October 7, 1946, the dedication was held. Inside the front door of the Sandburg house there was a framed note of tribute written about Carl Sandburg by Stephen Vincent Benét:

> He came to us from the people whom Lincoln loved because there were so many of them, and through all his life, in verse and prose, he has spoken of and for the people. A great American, we have just reason to be proud that he has lived and written in our time.

Sandburg's old friend Lloyd Lewis was writing a column at the time for the Chicago *Sun*, and he reported that Sandburg had reacted to the memorial by paraphrasing a remark of Cato's: "I would rather that people should some times, perhaps, suddenly and idly ask why there is no monument to me than why there is." Sandburg declined to attend the dedication. It was a long trip for the old man to make; besides, he felt it would seem immodest. But he told Lewis that he was grateful to the friends and admirers who had worked to create the memorial.

In 1948 the novel that had been begun on a large retainer from M-G-M was published. The huge book, *Remembrance Rock*, ran to 1,067 pages and traced the American adventure from Plymouth Rock to World War II, binding together what amounted to three regular-sized novels. It was about the ordeal of the Pilgrims, the American Revolution, and the Civil War and contained a heavy cataloguing of the comments, songs, sayings, and speeches of each era. These were devices Sandburg had used effectively in his Lincoln writings and in some of his poetry, such as *The People, Yes*.

Some of his old friends greeted Sandburg's first venture into adult fiction with kindliness. Fanny Butcher wrote in the Chicago *Tribune;* "It is the sum of everything Sandburg has written, learned, done." But elsewhere, among the nation's important critics, the novel was not well received. Diana Trilling concluded in *The Nation* that the novel was not worth reviewing. In *The New Yorker* it was called "passing dull," and *Time* Magazine termed it "the sort of novel a distinguished Supreme Court justice might write." The critic for *The Saturday Review of Literature* commented that "his portrayals of . . . American life are somehow static," and Perry Miller, in the lead article on the first page of *The New York Times Book Review*, said that "the book's orientation is not toward any philosophical thesis whatsoever, but toward a Hollywood production. . . ."

Sandburg was not disturbed by the critical attacks on his novel. It lay behind him. He had already begun to re-create his life in Galesburg for the first volume of his autobiography, which would not be completed for another five years.

Sandburg's *Complete Poems* (676 pages) was published by Harcourt, Brace and Company in 1950. Although it did not include the tyro work that had been published by Asgard Press, it did contain all of Sandburg's subsequent published work, as well as a section of new poems. For this volume of poetry, Sandburg was awarded his second Pulitzer Prize.

As his seventy-fifth birthday approached, Sandburg was awarded the Gold Medal in history and biography of the National Institute of Arts and Letters and the American Academy of Arts and Letters. On December 31, 1952, President Harry S. Truman wrote to Sandburg, "It's hard to reconcile reports that you will be seventy-five years old January sixth with those of your ringing participation in the November Democratic Rally at Madison Square Garden. You have my congratulations, however, upon your birthday and my thanks for helping Americans see their forefathers, their cities, their farms and themselves a little more clearly."

And that he was to do, even more admirably, in his autobiography, *Always the Young Strangers*, published on his seventy-fifth birthday, January 6, 1953. Of it, Robert E. Sherwood wrote in *The New York Times Book Review* on January 4; "At the risk of being convicted of hyperbole—the blackest crime of the reviewers' code—I feel compelled to put my neck in the noose with the statement that

lburg on his seventy-fifth birthday at the Blackstone Hotel in Chicago,
, with his wife, Paula.

'Always the Young Strangers' is, to me, the best autobiography ever written by an American." To read Sandburg's recollection of his life from his birth until he went off to serve in the Spanish-American War is to relive the life of Galesburg and small-town Midwestern America in the eighties and nineties.

The Illinois State Historical Society devoted its *Journal* that winter of 1952–53 to Carl Sandburg. There were tributes by Adlai Stevenson, historian Allan Nevins, Professor Quincy Wright (the son of Philip Green Wright), and numerous other friends, historians, and writers. On the night of Sandburg's seventy-fifth birthday, 550 of his friends, colleagues, and admirers attended a testimonial dinner for him in the Blackstone Hotel in Chicago. Sherwood and Nevins were among the guests, and Adlai Stevenson, then governor of Illinois, sent a recorded message, which said, in part, "He is in the earthiness of the prairies, the majesty of mountains, the anger of deep inland seas. In him is the restlessness of the seeker, the questioner, the explorer of far horizons, the hunger that is never satisfied." Erik Boheman was there as the representative of King Gustav VI Adolf of Sweden to bestow on Sandburg the honor of Swedish Commander of the Order of the Northern Star as "one of Sweden's prominent sons." And his brother-in-law, Edward Steichen, said, "On the day that God made Carl, He didn't do anything else that day but sit around and feel good."

Sandburg, accompanied by his wife, Paula, accepted this praise as spiritedly as ever. "If I were sixty-five, such an evening would be difficult to take," he said. "If I were fifty-five it would be impossible and if I were forty-five it would be unthinkable. But at seventy-five you become a trifle mellow and learn to go along with what true friends consider just homage."

That year, too, he made a sentimental return to Galesburg to visit many of his old friends, some of them for the last time. He would have been pleased to know what a clerk in a Galesburg cigar store replied when asked what the town's biggest industry was. "Carl Sandburg," she said.

In 1954, Ernest Hemingway was awarded the Nobel Prize for Literature. When reporters questioned him about his reaction to the honor, he said that Carl Sandburg deserved it more than he did. This pleased Sandburg immensely, and later that year, when he was attending the National Book Awards ceremony in New York, he told Harvey Breit of *The New York Times Book Review*, "Harvey Breit, I want to

Carl Sandburg at seventy-seven, 1955.

Sandburg recalls his first visit to Chicago sixty-one years ago.

Returning to the "Windy City" for Chicago Dynamic Week, he gazes at the skyscrapers of which he had written so profusely.

TOP   *Sandburg examines a model of the Carl Sandburg Village for Chicago.
Left to right: George H. Dovenmuelle, Mr. Rubloff, J. G. Duba, Sandburg,
Louis R. Solomon and J. D. Cordwell, May, 1962.*

BOTTOM   *During Chicago Dynamic Week, Clifford F. Hood, president of
U. S. Steel (left), and Sandburg present Mayor Richard J. Daley with the
Chicago Testament plaque.*

Frank Lloyd Wright and Carl Sandburg meet for the first time in 1957 for TV's Chicago Dynamic Hour.

tell you something, that sometime thirty years from now when the Breit boys are sitting around, one boy will say, 'Did Carl Sandburg ever win the Nobel Prize?' and one Breit boy will say, 'Ernest Hemingway gave it to him in 1954.' "

With the first installment of his autobiography behind him, Sandburg told interviewers that he was hard at work on the next section, which would cover his years of wandering, his days as a student of Professor Wright, his experience as a Socialist organizer, and his early writing efforts. It would be called "On the Wings of Chance," he said.

That year his distillation of his six-volume study of Lincoln was published in one 800-page edition, *Abraham Lincoln: The Prairie Years and the War Years*. This volume, he was to say, was perhaps his favorite prose work, the essence of all he had tried to say about Lincoln. That year, too, Sandburg journeyed to New York to receive the Silver Medal of the New York Civil War Round Table, which hailed him as "the Lincoln of our literature." He found time in his remarks to the Round Table to defend goat's milk and cheese from the scurrilous charge that they tasted bad.

He also attempted a task he enjoyed immensely—commenting on our Presidents as an elder statesman of history: "Theodore Roosevelt was a tremendous figure. He was the first to use the phrase 'malefactors of great wealth'—rich, ignorant, predatory men." Woodrow Wilson and Franklin D. Roosevelt might also be ranked "nearly on an equal with Lincoln." He added that "no one can go into that office and accomplish anything without being diabolically cunning," a trait that Lincoln, Washington, Jefferson, Theodore Roosevelt, Wilson, and Franklin Roosevelt shared, "or they couldn't have lasted."

In 1955, Sandburg wrote a foreword for Steichen's great collection of photographs entitled *Family of Man*. The following year he sold to the University of Illinois, for $30,000, a great part of his library of books, manuscripts, personal papers, and priceless Lincoln letters. *The Sandburg Range*, an anthology of Sandburg's writings, was published in 1957, and Sandburg visited Chicago for the Chicago Association of Commerce and Industry to help promote Chicago Dynamic Week. He would not have written so much about Chicago, he said, "if I had not loved Chicago as Victor Hugo loved his Paris, as Charles Lamb loved his London."

Sandburg was often in demand in these years as a celebrity. Magazines featured spreads of photographs documenting his visit with

Carl Sandburg and the skyscrapers.

actress Marilyn Monroe, and the old poet even danced a few steps with her. He toured the Gettysburg battlefield for a television special, read his poetry on the *Ed Sullivan Show*, and read more poetry on another television special while Gene Kelly danced an interpretation of the muscular verse. A dozen or more schools were named for him.

Sandburg celebrated his eightieth birthday in 1958, and as usual, the reporters visited him to hear his views on life. "It's inevitable, it's inexorable, it's written in the book of fate," he said, "that I die at an age divisible by eleven," because two of his great-grandfathers and a grandfather had died at such an age. He had recently recovered from a bout of flu, which had cut into his working time, but he said that he was no longer beset by "high anxiety" to keep writing. "But I'll keep producing. I'll probably die propped up in bed trying to write a poem about America. Or about a man who prayed that he could live to an age divisible by eleven."

He was not alarmed about growing old. "Death begins the moment the little fetus begins to shape itself; death is interwoven with life at all times." He added, "Age is relative. I've got a younger heart than most of the poets. Three-fourths of the poets we have nowadays were born old."

By February, 1958, he had recovered sufficiently to journey to Stateville Prison in Joliet, Illinois, where he appeared at a hearing before the state parole board to plead for the release of the state's most notorious prisoner. Thirty-four years before, in Chicago, Nathan Leopold had been convicted and sentenced to life imprisonment with Richard Loeb for the so-called thrill slaying of Bobby Franks. Attorney Elmer Gertz, shepherd of lost causes and a longtime friend of Sandburg's, was representing Leopold. Sandburg told the board that if Leopold were paroled, "I would be willing to have him in my house. I haven't the slightest fear of the impulses there may have been in him originally."

When a newspaperman acquaintance chided Sandburg as a bleeding heart for his support of Leopold's bid for freedom, Sandburg said, "There are those who won't like it, those who believe in revenge. They are the human stuff of which mobs are made. . . . I say . . . I don't have the mob-consciousness."

In his plea Sandburg said, "I have done my best. I have made a free confession. I am an Illinois boy of Knox County. I never thought it would get to the time I would make a winter morning journey to

Joliet to face the Board of Paroles, to plead for a Chicago Jewish boy who at nineteen was out of his mind." Leopold was, he said, "a struggler, a rather magnificent struggler. I would rather have been in prison and made a struggle than be Dave Beck or Jimmy Hoffa."

In time, Leopold was freed, and he has made an exemplary success of his parole. Later that year, however, Sandburg made a similar appeal on behalf of an aging, ailing friend—the poet Ezra Pound—but this effort was in vain. Pound, who had remained in Italy in World War II and supported the Fascist cause, was being held in St. Elizabeths Hospital for the Mentally Disturbed in Washington, D. C., and Sandburg was one of the distinguished poets and writers who petitioned the government for the great poet's liberty.

Later in 1958, Sandburg told a reporter that he was "half done" with the next installment of his autobiography. He would finish it, he said, in: "Let's say 1960. There are fellows who just start and plow right through. But I'm getting to the point where I have to make the explanation that all good autobiographers must make—that they're dirty liars if they say they are telling the truth, the whole truth and nothing but the truth."

On the one hundred and fiftieth anniversary of the birth of Lincoln, Sandburg became the second private citizen in history to address a joint session of Congress (the first had been historian George Bancroft, who had delivered a eulogy to President Lincoln). After actor Fredric March read the Gettysburg Address, House Speaker Sam Rayburn introduced the poet as "the man who in all probability knows more about the life, the times, the hopes and the aspirations of Abraham Lincoln than any other human being . . . this great historian, this great writer. . . ."

Sandburg spoke for twenty minutes. First, he quoted Lincoln's letter to those who had sought his help in raising a marble monument to his beloved friend Representative Owen Lovejoy of Illinois, who died in May, 1864: "Let him have the marble monument along with the well-assured and more enduring one on the hearts of those who love liberty, unselfishly, for all men."

Then Sandburg said, "Today we may say, perhaps, that the well-assured and most enduring memorial to Lincoln is invisibly there, today, tomorrow, and for a long time yet to come. It is there in the hearts of lovers of liberty, men and women—this country has always had them

"I would have him [Leopold], on the basis of numerous reports I consider unquestionable, as a guest in my home, whose companionship would be valued."

Before the Illinois state pardon and parole board in Stateville Penitentiary as witness for Nathan Leopold, 1958. Elmer Gertz (foreground) represented Leopold. Sandburg, whose friendship with Gertz dates back to the 1920's, said of Gertz, "He fears no dragons."

Vice-President Richard Nixon, Sandburg, and House Speaker Sam Rayburn. "Not often in the story of mankind does a man arrive who is both steel and velvet . . ." said Sandburg of Lincoln.

Poets Robert Frost and Carl Sandburg with Librarian of Congress L. Quincy L. Mumford (right) in Washington on the evening in 1960 when Sandburg received the Silver Laurel Wreath of the U. S. Chamber of Commerce.

Fame has not decreased Sandburg's feeling for the working man or less-
ened his strong support of labor. Here he discusses labor with Chicago
Federation of Labor's president William A. Lee (center) and author Harry
Golden.

ON FOLLOWING DOUBLE PAGE *President Kennedy and Sandburg enjoy a*
joke together, October 25, 1961. Sandburg was in Washington to open the
centennial exhibit of the Civil War for the Library of Congress.

in crisis—men and women who understand that wherever there is freedom there have been those who fought, toiled and sacrificed for it."

That year, too, a stage production of Sandburg's writings, *The World of Carl Sandburg*, opened in Portland, Maine. Actor Gary Merrill, who bore a strong resemblance to the poet, and his wife, actress Bette Davis, read the writings of Sandburg in an offering that was directed by Norman Corwin. It was not successful on Broadway as a dramatic venture, but—perhaps this is a tribute to Sandburg's reputation, as well as to that of Miss Davis and of Merrill—it enjoyed a successful tour.

During the busy year of 1959, Sandburg made his pilgrimage to the villages of his parents in Sweden. Before Sweden, he had visited Russia with Edward Steichen for the opening of the photographer's "Family of Man" exhibit. The audiences Sandburg enjoyed in Sweden, in personal appearances and on television, were proof of his great popularity there.

Sandburg was pleased with the Democratic Party platform of 1960, when John F. Kennedy was elected President. "That's a very good imitation of the national Socialist Party platform adopted in Chicago in 1908 when my wife and I were in sparking attendance," he said. After Kennedy had been in office for nearly a year, Sandburg said of him, "The chances are entirely that he's going to rate as one of the great Presidents. He's a great relief from the press conferences of Dwight David Eisenhower, the most ungrammatical President we've ever had. Shooting off about the Youth [Peace] Corps: Before it's begun to have a tryout he says it's no use. That wasn't good sportsmanship. He has yet to know the people of the United States. With him the words 'socialist' and 'socialism' are dirty words. Very nearly as dirty as 'welfare state.' But ever since he left the creamery of Abilene, Kansas, he never bought a suit of clothes or a meal, he never was out of work for a day. All the anxieties that go with the free enterprise system, he's never known them. He's lived in a welfare state ever since he left Abilene and went to West Point."

"On the showing so far," Sandburg said in October, 1961, in a visit to the White House, where he paid his respects to the President, "Mr. Kennedy looks as if he might become a great President." Sandburg was eighty-three then, and he did not know that he was to outlive the youthful President and see that bright promise shattered by outrageous violence.

178

Actress Bette Davis and actor Gary Merrill relax with Carl after the pre-miere of Norman Corwin's The World of Carl Sandburg *in Portland, Maine, October 13, 1959.*

Sandburg and actress Ingrid Bergman were both in a movie called Swedes in America, *made in Hollywood for Sweden in 1943.*

Sandburg mugs with comedian Milton Berle in the Beverly Hills Hotel, 1958.

Actress Elizabeth Taylor and Carl Sandburg each played a part in the making of the movie version of The Greatest Story Ever Told.

Sandburg, age eighty-six, receives the Presidential Freedom Medal from President Johnson in a White House ceremony, September 14, 1964. Major General Chester Clifton, the President's military aide, holds the medal.

Carl Sandburg

Although Sandburg was limiting his activities as the infirmities of age began to trouble him, the nation was not forgetting him. In 1964, President Lyndon B. Johnson presented the nation's Freedom Medal to the old poet for his contribution to the American people's understanding of their land and its history. The following year Sandburg was the first white person to receive the Medal of Honor of the National Association for the Advancement of Colored People as "a leading prophet for civil rights in our time."

On Sandburg's eighty-eighth birthday, in 1966, President Johnson sent a telegram to congratulate him and said, "Thanks to you, the people live on with a deeper insight into their nation, their fellow citizens, and their own inherent dignity."

FACING PAGE *Of the People . . .*

I O

The Closing Stanza

FEW are the American writers who mature, grow, and deepen with age. Most flare in brief glorious radiance and then, with a lovely fading light, burn themselves out, fleeting candles to be celebrated for their unfulfilled promise.

William Faulkner, Robert Frost, and Carl Sandburg defy this pattern, for they share a silent understanding with time. They would not attempt to rush the minutes and the hours and the years if time, in its turn, would permit them the luxury of developing and creating according to their own sure and steady pace.

Sandburg's first major publication of poetry came when he was thirty-eight. *The Prairie Years* was not published until he was nearly fifty, and *The War Years* came out when he was sixty-one. But this was in accordance with the long, slow coming of age of a writer who was not certain of his path until he was well into his young manhood. Once he had found his way, Sandburg's productive years lengthened into nearly half a century.

It almost looked as if the flow would never cease, but, of course, that could not happen. Ultimately, time must prevail. That is part of the bargain. Although in recent years Sandburg continued to speak of a desire to write, he seemed finally to have exhausted his resources. He spoke of a second installment of his autobiography. He told friends he would like to write a "small book" about Lincoln's self-education,

Modern bust of Carl Sandburg by Hal Schor.

Sandburg listens to Supreme Court Justice William O. Douglas at his eighty-fifth birthday celebration.

Every day when he was feeling well, Sandburg would write, still wearing the green eyeshade.

and perhaps in the back of his mind there was that dream of a great Jefferson biography. But with the exception of a last small collection of poems, *Honey and Salt,* which appeared on his eighty-fifth birthday, none of his later ambitions was achieved.

Yet every day, when he was feeling good, Sandburg wrote in his white frame mansion in North Carolina. He still wore the green eyeshade he began to use in his newspaper days. It had become a fixture in his life. Eyeshades were scattered around his house so that one was at hand wherever he decided to settle—to read or to write.

He spoke of the approach of death calmly, almost affectionately, as of an old friend. It was the attitude we would expect of a man who all his life had lived as if he had understood and accepted the compact with time. In his final years, when the reporters came on his birthday to speak with him, he liked to repeat what he had written in the Preface to his *Complete Poems* in 1950: "It could be, in the Grace of God, I shall live to be eighty-nine, as did Hokusai, and speaking my farewell to earthly scenes, I might paraphrase: 'If God had let me live five years longer I should have been a writer.'"

With his creative years at an end, Sandburg must now become the property of the future. Posterity alone will determine his place in literature. It is deceptively easy to think of Sandburg as a predictable artist who can easily be assigned to his niche. Everyone understands Sandburg.

But which Sandburg? The radical young agitator whose social sentiments found a voice in poetry? The controversial poet who dipped into the common font of language and experience to create a new rhetoric of poetry which unsettled quite a few traditionalist critics? The biographer who leveled the poet's eye on barren facts to clothe them in truth? The historian who gave us, not only the chronicle, but also the texture, of a complex era in a narrative of such clarity that anyone should be able to comprehend it? The autobiographer who seemed to possess a magical ability to project himself backward in time, so detailed was his reminiscence?

On the other hand, it may be said of Sandburg that his radical social and political notions became commonplace after Franklin Roosevelt. Free verse? Merely a pause between traditional poetry and the wave of the future, already augured in the time of Sandburg's brief reign as a controversial poet by the rise of Pound and Eliot and Cummings. The twenties and after made Sandburg's tough talk seem almost

190

Calmly, he spoke of the approach of death.

"*Master of Free Verse,*" 1943.

As a witness before a special Senate subcommittee, Sandburg testifies for a proposed universal copyright law.

Carl Sandburg

naïve. And since Sandburg's Lincoln achievements, the writing of biography and history has achieved such a high professional gloss as the world has never seen.

And where were the mystery and the depth of Sandburg? Essentially, wasn't he another yea-sayer in an era when the vogue was to say nay? Where was the evidence of the impact of Freud and Jung in his writings? Wasn't his a voice left over from the Industrial Revolution, raised to combat the sins of an America which no longer existed? Where is his relevance to our times, that lasting significance which is the dividend literature must pay if it is to achieve greatness?

Contemporary critics have scorned or ignored Sandburg because his poetry was always posing questions and never supplying any answers. In terms of his social protest, this was patently untrue. Intrinsic in all his poetry of protest were the remedies for our social ills, and like a successful prophet, Sandburg lived to see most of them administered. But what about the questions of man's identity, his role in the universe, the meaning of his fraction of a fraction of a second against the eons of unrecordable time? Certainly Sandburg has given us no answers here, and just as certainly no other poet or philosopher has answered them. Some have created frameworks around a portion of the void and told us: "Here, this is the place to make your stand." Perhaps there is more honesty in Sandburg's refusal to pretend that there is something where there is probably nothing. There is, in fact, a forerunning theme of existentialism in his writing, in his acceptance of the human condition and his decision to seek the glory of man in it.

Modern critics seem to resent Sandburg's intelligibility. Anyone can interpret Sandburg, so what does that leave the modern critic to do? Without obscurantism, an entire school of literary criticism might have to return to book reviewing. But does saying something with greater obscurity give it any greater depth?

Some critics, too, seem to resent Sandburg's popularity. How can a poet or a writer be any good if the people like him? Literary reputations should be left in the hands of critics and professors, not the reading public.

There is some truth in both laudatory and critical approaches to Sandburg. Much of his poetry—some critics seem to think most of his poetry by the way they are eschewing it now in recent anthologies—has become outdated. Its novelty, its controversial aspects, and its timeliness have passed, and it cannot survive without them. Certainly

194

Sandburg had great admiration for the "good fool" who leavened even life's most serious moments with wit, as Abraham Lincoln had done.

Late in life he wrote, with almost total recall, his classic autobiography, Always the Young Strangers. *It is the story of his life up to the turn of the century.*

A silent understanding with time.

his one novel, *Remembrance Rock,* cannot survive except as a literary curiosity. His *Rootabaga Stories* and their successors seem to have little appeal for our sophisticated modern children.

But some of his poems will endure, not as exhibits of literary history, but upon the merits of freshness and strength of language, and because of the celebration of the glory of American democracy, and love for man and for the world.

And the autobiography, *Always the Young Strangers,* should become a classic of its kind. It is impossible to think of another evocation of life in small-town America before the turn of the century that succeeds more admirably than Sandburg's in re-creating that vanished time before the technological revolution freed the farmboys from the land and destroyed the essence of the little market towns. It is written with such a charming clarity and such a feeling of honesty that perhaps it captures the truth about small-town America better than novels such as Sherwood Anderson's *Winesburg, Ohio.* For Winesburg was only a dark corner among the thousand Galesburgs.

And what of Sandburg's Lincoln? Which judgment of it shall prevail, that of critic Edmund Wilson—who wrote in *Patriotic Gore,* "There are moments when one is tempted to feel that the cruelest thing that has happened to Lincoln since he was shot by Booth was to fall into the hands of Carl Sandburg"—or that of the myriad other critics who have hailed Sandburg's achievement as a pinnacle of historical biography which may never be reached again?

Surely his Lincoln shall endure. Although Wilson resents the sentimental proprietorship Sandburg displays toward Lincoln, who else can ever perform the feat of research and writing that Sandburg accomplished with *Abraham Lincoln: The Prairie Years and The War Years?* Until Sandburg succeeded, no historian had managed to get beneath the heroic image of Lincoln to reveal the true man inside the icon. Sandburg has given us a far more fascinating and memorable portrait of the man called Lincoln than we ever had. And no one else can ever again bring to a Lincoln biography the kind of authenticity that Sandburg was able to achieve because the world of the Illinois prairie is gone.

It is fitting that the old poet, the long-ago radical, the renowned biographer of Lincoln, and the beloved re-creator of a vanished America lived to enjoy a long harvest after so many years of labor. Illness troubled him in recent years. His daughter Helga described movingly one such critical bout of peritonitis in the late winter of

1966. Sandburg was hospitalized, and when his family visited him, he was unable to recognize his daughter or her husband. He sat repeating the tales he loved to tell, which he had told them so often, of his boyhood in Galesburg and of the people he had met in his vagabond years, of Lincoln and of his love for his wife of more than half a century. And he sang the songs of the people, which he loved and many of which probably owe their survival as part of our folk heritage to him.

In June, 1967, the poet suffered his first heart attack. For six weeks he lay in his bed in the plain house of hand-hewn timbers, where from his bedroom windows he could gaze through the pine trees to the mountains that this man of the Illinois prairies had come to love. He was stricken by a second heart attack in mid-July, and early on Saturday, July 22, his beloved Paula reported that he had died peacefully in his sleep.

The news of the tragedy swiftly circled the globe. Suddenly, people who had perhaps not thought of Carl Sandburg in many years felt the sense of inexplicable loss that only a few public figures inspire. World leaders, poets and writers and critics, and the "People" that Sandburg loved tried to find words to phrase their eulogies. But let President Lyndon Johnson's memorial suffice to state what so many found inexpressible:

> The road has come to an end for Carl Sandburg, my friend and the good companion of millions, whose own life's journeys have been ennobled and enriched by his poetry.
>
> But there is no end to the legacy he leaves us.
>
> Carl Sandburg was more than the voice of America, more than the poet of its strength and genius. He was America. We knew and cherished him as the bard of democracy, the echo of the people, our conscience, and chronicler of truth and beauty and purpose.
>
> Carl Sandburg needs no epitaph. It is written for all time in the fields, the cities, the face and heart of the land he loved, and the people he celebrated and inspired.
>
> With the world we mourn his passing. It is our special pride and fortune as Americans that we will always hear Carl Sandburg's voice within ourselves. For he gave us the truest and most enduring vision of our own greatness.

Paula Sandburg spoke the final epitaph when after her husband's passing she repeated the words that Edwin M. Stanton, Secretary of War under Lincoln, spoke after his President had died: "Now he belongs to the ages."

Sandburg receives the Order of the Northern Star with the rank of commander from Erik Boheman, Swedish Ambassador to the United States, on Carl Sandburg Day, Chicago, January 6, 1953.

Returning, once again, to Chicago.

ABOVE *With a child's heart, he reads from the* Rootabaga Stories.
OPPOSITE *Carl Sandburg in Stockholm, August 13, 1959.*

OPPOSITE   *He thumbs his nose when reporters asked him to give them an unusual picture with which they could impress their editors, August 20, 1957, in the half-constructed Morton Salt Company's building.*

ABOVE   *Sandburg, age seventy-three, admires one of his prize goats, Cloey, held by his granddaughter, Karen Paula Thoman, age seven, at Connemara, North Carolina, June 27, 1951.*

A laugh.

A prayer.

Paula and her "Buddy" in their North Carolina home.

Selected Bibliography

Barnard, Harry, *Eagle Forgotten*. Indianapolis, Bobbs-Merrill Co., 1938.

Bradley, Dr. Preston, *Along the Way*. New York, David McKay Co., 1962.

Crowder, Richard, *Carl Sandburg*. New York, Twayne Publishers, 1964.

De Oliveras, Jose, *Our Islands and Their People*. New York, N. D. Thompson Publishing Co., 1899.

Detzer, Karl, *Carl Sandburg: A Study in Personality and Background*. New York, Harcourt, Brace, 1941.

Duffey, Bernard, *The Chicago Renaissance in American Letters: A Critical History*. East Lansing, Michigan State University Press, 1954.

Durnell, Hazel, *The America of Carl Sandburg*. Seattle, University of Washington Press, 1966.

Gertz, Elmer, *A Handful of Clients*. Chicago, Follett Publishing Co., 1965.

Golden, Harry, *Carl Sandburg*. Cleveland, World Publishing Co., 1961.

Hansen, Harry, *Midwest Portraits*. New York, Harcourt, Brace, 1923.

Hecht, Ben, *A Child of the Century*. New York, Simon and Schuster, 1954.

Illinois State Historical Society Journal, XLV (1952). Carl Sandburg issue, with articles by Alfred Harcourt, Allan Nevins, Adlai Stevenson, Robert E. Sherwood, and others.

Knox College, *Knox Directory*. Galesburg, Publicity and Alumni Office, 1966.

Monroe, Harriet, "Carl Sandburg." *Poetry: A Magazine of Verse* (September, 1924).

Monroe, Harriet, *Poets and Their Art*. New York, Macmillan, 1926.

Parry, Albert, *Garrets and Pretenders: A History of Bohemianism in America*, rev. ed. New York, Dover Books, 1960.

Selected Bibliography

Sandburg, Carl, *Abraham Lincoln: The Prairie Years*. New York, Harcourt, Brace, 1926.

———, *Abraham Lincoln: The War Years*. New York, Harcourt, Brace, 1939.

———, *Always the Young Strangers*. New York, Harcourt, Brace, 1953.

———, *The American Songbag*. New York, Harcourt, Brace, 1927.

———, *The Chicago Race Riots, July, 1919*. New York, Harcourt, Brace and Howe, 1919.

———, *Complete Poems*. New York, Harcourt, Brace, 1950.

———, *The People, Yes*. New York, Harcourt, Brace, 1936.

———, *The Sandburg Range*. New York, Harcourt, Brace, 1957.

Schorer, Mark, *Sinclair Lewis: An American Way of Life*. New York, McGraw-Hill, 1961.

Smith, Henry Justin, *Deadlines: Being the Quaint, the Amusing, the Tragic Memoirs of a Newsroom*. Chicago, Covici-McGee, 1923.

Index

Index

* Italicized page numbers refer to illustrations.

215

Index

Index

Index

Index